Intercultural
Business
Communication

Also published in
Oxford Handbooks for Language Teachers

Teaching American English Pronunciation
Peter Avery and Susan Ehrlich

Success in English Teaching
Paul Davies and Eric Pearse

Teaching Business English
Mark Ellis and Christine Johnson

Teaching and Learning in the Language Classroom
Tricia Hedge

Teaching English Overseas: An Introduction
Sandra Lee McKay

Teaching English as an International Language
Sandra Lee McKay

How Languages are Learned
Patsy M. Lightbown and Nina Spada

Communication in the Language Classroom
Tony Lynch

Explaining English Grammar
George Yule

Intercultural
Business
Communication

Robert Gibson

OXFORD
UNIVERSITY PRESS

OXFORD
UNIVERSITY PRESS

Great Clarendon Street, Oxford ox2 6dp

Oxford University Press is a department of the University
of Oxford. It furthers the University's objective of excellence
in research, scholarship, and education by publishing
worldwide in

Oxford New York

Auckland   Bangkok   Buenos Aires   Cape Town   Chennai
Dar es Salaam   Delhi   Hong Kong   Istanbul   Karachi   Kolkata
Kuala Lumpur   Madrid   Melbourne   Mexico City   Mumbai   Nairobi
São Paulo   Shanghai   Singapore   Taipei   Tokyo   Toronto

with an associated company in Berlin

© Cornelsen & Oxford University Press GmbH & Co. 2000
First published by Cornelsen & Oxford University Press GmbH & Co as Studium Kompakt:
Intercultural Business Communication by Robert Gibson.

This international edition was first published in 2002 and is not
available in Germany and Austria.

Database right Oxford University Press (maker)

isbn 0 19 442180 5

Printed in Spain by Unigraf, S.L.

CONTENTS

ACKNOWLEDGEMENTS

Many of the ideas discussed in this book originate from leading figures in the field. As will soon become clear some sources dominate—they include Edward Hall, who has been active from the late 1950s, Geert Hofstede, famous for his groundbreaking quantitative studies, as well as Fons Trompenaars, who has done so much to popularize the subject. Thanks must also go to the interculturalists in SIETAR (the Society for Intercultural Education, Training and Research) and ENCoDE (the European Network for Communication Development in Business and Education) who have so generously shared their ideas at numerous congresses and workshops. I am also indebted to the students at Ingolstadt School of Business and its international partner institutions, as well as to Interkulturelle Management Beratung Dr. Gnann, and my colleagues at Siemens.

Robert Gibson

The author and publisher are grateful to those who have given permission to reproduce the following extracts and adaptations of copyright material:

Automotive News Europe for permission to reproduce 'Culture clash at D/C worse than expected' by Dorothee Ostle. *Automotive News Europe* 22 November 1999. © Crain Communications Ltd.

Blackwell Publishers for permission to reproduce an extract from *Intercultural Communication* by Ron Scollon and S. Wong Scollon, 1995.

Nicholas Brealey Publishing for permission to reproduce extracts from *Riding the Waves of Culture* 2nd Ed. by F. Trompenaars and C. Hampden-Turner (1998); from *When Cultures Collide* by R. Lewis (1996); and from *Breaking Through Culture Shock* by E. Marx (1999).

Dennis Clackworthy and Siemens for permission to reproduce 'Business determinants and cultural determinants' and p. 00 'A road map to cultural competency' by Dennis Clackworthy (Siemens Review 2/94).

Nicholas Coleridge for permission to reproduce 'We have ways of making you work' by Nicholas Coleridge, *Sunday Telegraph* 30 August 1998.

Doubleday, a division of Random House Inc. for permission to reproduce an extract from *Beyond Culture* by Edward T. Hall, copyright © 1976, 1981 by Edward T. Hall.

Faber and Faber Ltd. For permission to reproduce an extract from 'Little Gidding' from *Four Quartets* by T. S. Eliot. From *Collected Poems 1909–1962.*

Geert Hofstede for permission to reproduce extracts from *Cultures and Organizations* by Geert Hofstede © Geert Hofstede.

Intercultural Press for permission to reproduce an extract from *The Art of Crossing Cultures* and an extract from *Cross Cultural Dialogues* by Craig Storti.

Kogan Page for permission to reproduce an extract from *Managing Cultural Diversity* at Work by Khizar Humayun Ansari and June Jackson (1995).

Nihon Keizai Shimbun for permission to reproduce an extract from *16 Ways to Avoid Saying No* by Masaaki Imai © 1981 Masaaki Imai. All rights reserved.

Pearson Education for permission to reproduce an extract from *Managing Cultural Differences* by Lisa Hoecklin (1995) and from *Negotiating* by Philip O'Connor, Adrian Pilbeam, and Fiona Scott-Barrett.

Procter and Gamble for permission to reproduce the Procter and Gamble Statement on Diversity.

Routledge for permission to reproduce an extract from *Culture Shock* by Adrian Furnham and Stephen Bochner.

Sage Publications for permission to reproduce an extract from *Intercultural Communication* by Fred E. Jandt, and an extract from Harry Triandis in *Cross Cultural Perspectives on Learning* edited by Richard W. Brislin, Stephen Bochner, and Walter J. Lonner. (eds.) © 1975 Sage Publications Inc.

SIETAR for permission to reproduce an extract from N. Garratt-Gnann et. al. in *Images, Cultures and Communications* by Cruzeby et. al. and extracts from *Managing Intercultural Negotiations* by P. Casse and S. Deol; extracts from Marie-Therese Claes and M. Pauwels in *Heritage and Progress: from the Past to the Future in Intercultural Understanding* edited by D. Lynch and A. Pilbeam; an extract from 'Teaming with trouble – Konfliktpoteniale in deutsch-amerikanischen Teams' by H. Robinson and R. Wuebbeler, *SIETAR Deutschland Newsletter* 1/2000; an extract from 'The uneasy road to successful cross-border co-operations and mergers' by M. Fischer. *SIETAR Europa Newsletter* 1/2000.

Wirtschaftsverlag Carl Ueberreuter GmbH for permission to reproduce an extract from *Wirtschaftspartner zwischen Wunsch und Wirklichkeit* by Reisach, Tauber and Yaun © Wirtschaftsverlag Carl Ueberreuter GmbH, 60439 Frankfurt am Main, Germany. All rights reserved.

INTRODUCTION

'Intercultural communication' has become one of the 'hottest' labels of our times, but more and more people are becoming aware of the fact that 'soft skills' are no substitute for technical know-how, and that without that knowledge they have little chance of succeeding in the global village.

This book aims to provide those involved with business communication with an introduction to this fascinating interdisciplinary field. Chapter 1 looks at the why, what, and how of Intercultural Communication, Chapter 2 provides a survey of some key cultural dimensions, while Chapter 3 focuses on the intercultural aspect of communication skills that business people need to function effectively at work. Chapter 4 includes examples from a selection of cultures of special interest to the business community. The final section, Chapter 5, provides hints on ways of training people to develop intercultural skills, as well as a bibliography and a glossary of key terms.

The approach is interactive, with exercises that encourage readers to reflect on their own attitudes and experience, before comparing their answers to those suggested in the book. The aim is to introduce readers to the subject, to supplement rather than replace their own experience, reflection, and training.

How to use *Intercultural Business Communication*

Special features of the book include:

Recycling of key concepts The cultural dimensions presented in Chapter 2 provide a basis for the treatment of the business communication functions presented in Chapter 3, and the specific cultures dealt with in Chapter 4. If you work through the whole book you will find that your knowledge of these key concepts is reinforced as you go.

Exercises help you to relate your own experience to the ideas presented in the book. To benefit from them fully it is important to be as honest as you can when doing them. Note down keywords before you look at the suggested answers in the Comments section. Remember that these are just suggestions; there are often no black and white answers.

Critical incidents are short descriptions of events which struck one or more participants as of particular importance; often things went wrong. They are either based on personal experience, or developed from research findings. Try to be as creative and open as possible in working out what happened. Use your own experience, as well as knowledge gained from working with *Intercultural Business Communication.*

Cultural checklists at the end of sections provide you with a brief summary of the main ideas covered. Instead of providing lists of dos and don'ts, these will often ask you questions, rather than provide you with the answers; they aim to suggest which areas to consider.

Further reading *Intercultural Business Communication* is an introduction to the field. This section gives you tips on materials which will help you to explore the particular area further.

Remember the words of an emperor of China:

> The people of the world are bigoted and unenlightened: invariably they regard what is like them as right, and what is different from them as wrong.
> They do not realise that the types of humanity are not uniform, that it is not only impossible to force people to become different but also impossible to force them to become alike.
>
> (Yung Cheng 1727)

Glossary Words in SMALL CAPITALS are explained in the Glossary on page 99.

1 THE INTERCULTURAL CHALLENGE

Why is intercultural communication important?

Exercise 1

An example

Extracts from a report on the DaimlerChrysler merger illustrate the importance of INTERCULTURAL communication.

What cultural problems do you think DaimlerChrysler had after their merger? What could they do about them?

Compare your ideas with those expressed in the article.

A German executive working for DaimlerChrysler recalled a meeting with US colleagues:

'When one of the Americans from Chrysler brought up what he thought was a new issue, a German counterpart said, "But we have agreed on this already in an earlier discussion. It is all written in the protocol." The American looked puzzled, and said, "What protocol? I remember you took some notes, and you sent me some papers recently, but I didn't think they were important."'

'At the beginning, one side tried to impose its working style on the other', said Roland Klein, DaimlerChrysler's manager of corporate communications in Stuttgart. 'This prompted conflicts and misunderstandings. But even worse, it just didn't fit with the people's culture.'

The Germans taking part were irritated by the Americans' unstructured ways, while the Americans thought the Germans were too rigid and formal. A senior product development executive in Stuttgart said that 'Each side thought its components or methods were the best.'

Klein said that there were fundamental differences between the executives in Chrysler and Daimler.

'Germans analyse a problem in great detail, find a solution, discuss it with their partners, and then make a decision. It's a very structured process', he said.

'Americans start with a discussion, and then come back to new aspects after talking with other people—after a process which they call creative—they come to a conclusion.' Former Daimler-Benz executives found the system chaotic. They were often puzzled by the American tendency to return to a subject they thought had been settled. Klein said that the two sides also decide things in different ways. In America, he said, 'At any time you can just pop into your boss's office and tell him something. The boss can make an instant decision—without explaining the reasons or involving other employees. It's different in Germany: the underlings prepare extensive reports for the top bosses and make recommendations at formal meetings.'

A high-ranking engineer in Auburn Hills said: '(At the old Chrysler) if an idea had merit, you didn't worry about approval, you just went ahead and did it. People working on the shop floor feel empowered to do things. It's based on management trust. Over there (in Germany) they've got all those smokestack organizations that measure things, survey things. A lot of time is spent on unproductive activities.' The clashing styles became apparent when Chrysler's US methods were adopted in purchasing operations in Germany. The American style was imposed largely because Chrysler executive Gary Valade heads DaimlerChrysler global purchasing. 'It just didn't work out over here', said Klein. 'There are some European suppliers which you have to approach differently, or even have to deal with in the German language. For Americans, this was a CULTURE SHOCK.' A senior product development executive in Germany said that top management probably underestimated the difficulties.
(Ostle, D. *Automotive News Europe*. 22.11.99)

Suggested answer
The cultural issues raised by this article include differences in the way decisions are made, communication style, the role of meetings, structure versus informality, management style, and the use of local language. These and many other aspects of intercultural communication are the subject matter of this book.

As it happens, DaimlerChrysler soon became aware of these problems, and since the merger has invested large amounts of money in preparing employees for intercultural interactions. Their 'Joint Program Germany–USA' focused on expatriates and their families (i.e. Germans working in the USA and Americans working in Germany), staff and managers who work regularly with American or German partners and German–American teams. Training included preparation for the foreign assignment, as well as leadership, negotiation, and language training.

Exercise 2
Reflect on any similar experiences of culture clash you have had, and how you dealt with them.

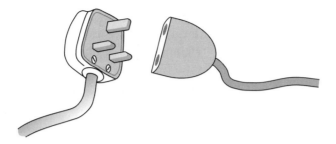

1 Where did the incident occur?
2 Who was involved?
3 What exactly happened?
4 What did you feel at the time?
5 How far do you think the incident was caused by cultural factors?
6 How has your behaviour changed since?

Business organization and culture

Now, more than ever before in human history, more people are coming into contact with people from cultures other than their own. There are a number of reasons for this:

- Technology makes it possible for people to travel further and faster than ever before.
- The internet links people across national boundaries.
- The international labour force is more mobile.
- More people are on the move than ever before: business people are active globally, refugees are trying to escape from conflicts and natural disasters.
- In many places the workforce is becoming more diverse.

Intercultural skills are not only needed by those involved with mega cross-border mergers, such as that of DaimlerChrysler, but by people working in all kinds of organizations. Even a domestic company which only operates in Germany, for instance, is faced with an increasingly multicultural workforce. A small or medium-sized enterprise in Munich, for instance, where non-Germans account for more than 20% of the population, may have workers with a wide range of cultural backgrounds (for example, German, Turkish, Serbian, Croatian, and Greek).

If the company wishes to grow, it may look beyond the domestic market and decide to export. For this, it will need to adapt its products or services for the foreign market, and negotiate with prospective partners abroad.

Somewhat surprisingly, if an organization relies on local structures when it becomes a multinational, the need for intercultural awareness may decline. The next stage of going global requires high-level skills to manage DIVERSITY inside and outside the company. The transnational organization develops into a 'global structure requiring networked multinational skills and abilities with a critical understanding of local responsiveness, integrating and coordinating mechanisms of corporate culture on a global basis' (Brake *et al.* 1995: 20).

Any given company may become involved in different kinds of intercultural interaction. Dennis Clackworthy identifies different 'cultural force fields' within the German electronics company Siemens concerning individuals, project teams, task forces, joint ventures, co-operation agreements, and global alliances (see Figure 1.1).

Business Determinants
influencing **what** is done

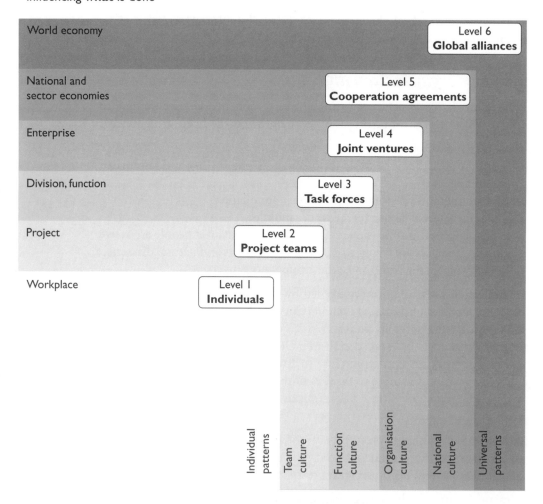

Figure 1.1: Business and cultural determinants (Clackworthy, personal communication)

To sum up, it is clear that managers in many companies will increasingly find themselves working in international teams at home, abroad, and in cyber-space, negotiating with foreign partners, and managing a diverse workforce.

Of course, intercultural communication is not only of importance for business people. Exercise 3 aims to help you reflect on some examples of how it could be important for other professionals.

Exercise 3

In what way could intercultural communication be important for the following people?

1 A doctor
2 An internet website designer
3 A university lecturer.

Suggested answer

1 *A doctor*

Attitudes to illness, kinds of treatment, the role of the doctor and his/her relationship towards the patient vary widely across cultures. What is considered an illness in one culture may not be seen as such in another. Some cultures favour treatment of the whole person, others concentrate on dealing with specific symptoms. In some cultures the doctor will put more emphasis on the patient as a person, while in others the focus is on analysing the illness.

2 *An internet website designer*

Although the internet has its origins in the USA, different cultures are now using it in different ways that suit their own environment and needs. Research comparing how the same company presents itself on the internet in different countries has revealed considerable cultural differences. One example is that some cultures prefer to use visual material and icons, while others favour more text. A designer has to take these sorts of factors into account if the communication is to be effective.

3 *A university lecturer*

A university lecturer working abroad, or with foreign students or a multi-cultural group at home, will have to be aware of a number of cultural issues. In the UK or USA, for instance, students may well call their professors by their first name, which in other cultures would be a sign of disrespect. The role of the teacher is different in different cultures. Western teachers working in Thailand, for example, complained that the students rarely asked questions in their classes, not realizing that it would be considered rude to ask questions, because this would imply that the teacher had not explained things satisfactorily in the first place. Forms of assessment vary—in some cultures, oral tests predominate, in others there are more written tests.

Synergy effects

The article about DaimlerChrysler (see p. 1 above) may confirm some people's belief that contact between cultures only brings problems. A production manager on the Anglo-French Concorde project said he felt that the product would have been better and considerably cheaper if either the French or the British had made the supersonic plane rather than working together. However, more and more companies see things much more positively, and are looking for and finding synergy effects in cultural diversity. SYNERGY (from the Greek for 'working together') means that the combined effect is more than the effect of the sum of the individual parts, i.e. 1+1 = 3. An example of this is the policy developed by Procter and Gamble. The extract below is taken from their statement on diversity:

Why is diversity important?

Developing and managing a strong, diverse organization is essential to achieving our business purpose and objectives.

- Our business opportunities are increasingly related to the entire world. And it is a diverse world. We must have the ability to deal with diverse consumers and customers in order to develop products and services of superior quality and value.
- Diversity provides for a broader, richer, more fertile environment for creative thinking and innovation.
- Because we see diversity as an asset, we will attract and develop talent from the full range of the world's rich cultural base. It is from this increasingly diverse pool of talent that our future leadership will come.

We value the different perspectives that the diversity of Procter and Gamble people bring to the business. Our workplace environment encourages collaboration which brings our different talents and experiences together to produce better ideas and superior services and products.

At Procter & Gamble, we operate on the fundamental belief that individual differences are good, and that such differences will produce genuine competitive advantage.

(Procter and Gamble)

What is intercultural communication?

Culture

There are a great many ways of defining the word CULTURE. In this book, culture is not used in the sense of literature, music, and art, but rather in the sense of a shared system of attitudes, beliefs, values, and behaviour. Hofstede has called it 'collective mental programming', or the 'software of the mind'. For some, it is simply 'the way we do things around here'.

Various models have been used to illustrate the concept. It can be seen as an iceberg, for instance, with the tangible expressions of culture and behaviour above the surface of the water, and the underlying attitudes, beliefs, values, and meanings below the surface. Depending on the individual's perspective, those involved in intercultural interactions could be on a cruise liner approaching the iceberg, or the *Titanic* about to crash into it.

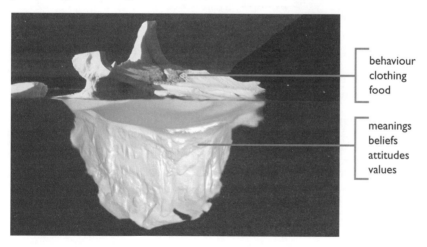

behaviour
clothing
food

meanings
beliefs
attitudes
values

The onion model sees layers of culture which can be peeled away to reveal underlying basic assumptions.

The tree model contrasts visible and hidden culture, with the roots providing an image of the historical origins of culture. Moving between cultures is like transplanting a tree—to be successful, the roots have to be protected, and support will be needed in the new environment.

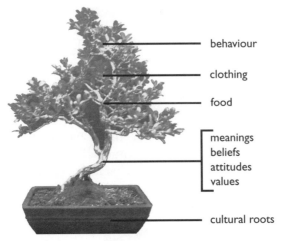

behaviour

clothing

food

meanings
beliefs
attitudes
values

cultural roots

Types of culture

When interculturalists use the word 'culture' they do not just mean national culture, but the whole range of different types of culture. These include:

- corporate culture (for example, the culture of Microsoft)
- professional culture (for example, the culture of lawyers or doctors)
- gender (the different cultures of men and women)
- age (the different cultures of young, middle-aged, and old people)
- religious culture (for example, Catholicism, Protestantism, Islam)
- regional culture (for example, Northern and Southern Italy)
- class culture (working class, middle class, and upper class).

In some cases these factors may play a more significant part than national culture in binding people together. Scientists of different nationalities who work together on research projects frequently report on how their common professional interests are so strong that national cultural differences become unimportant.

Intercultural communication

Communication can be defined as the exchange of meaning. This involves the sending and receiving of information between a SENDER and a RECEIVER. This happens not only through the use of words, but also through non-verbal factors, such as gestures and facial expression. The message received can be very different from the message that was sent. A common model for communication is shown in Figure 1.2.

The idea or feeling comes from the SOURCE. This is put into symbols (encoded) to produce a MESSAGE which is transmitted through a CHANNEL. The channel is the medium used for communication (for example, writing). The message is interpreted by the RECEIVER (decoded), who responds. The CONTEXT is the environment in which the communication takes place. 'noise' here means anything which distorts the message.

Intercultural communication takes place when the sender and the receiver are from different cultures. Communication can be very difficult if there is a big difference between the two cultures; if there is too much 'cultural noise', it can break down completely.

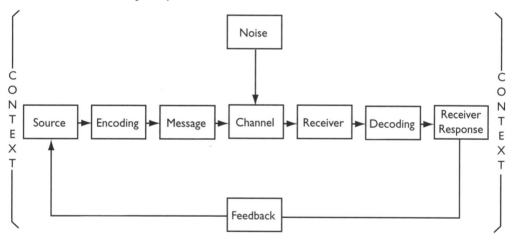

Figure 1.2: Communication model (Jandt 1995)

Barriers to intercultural communication

Attitude

Exercise 4

Comment on these statements:

1 Globalization means that there is now one business culture everywhere in the world.
2 If they want to do business with me, then they'll have to adapt to my culture.
3 'When in Rome, do as the Romans do.'
4 It's impossible to generalize about cultures—there are so many differences.
5 Intercultural training just confirms STEREOTYPES.
6 Today I'm dealing with the Americans, tomorrow with a group from Japan. I can't possibly learn all I need to know about all the cultures I have to deal with.
7 What I need when I go abroad is a list of dos and don'ts.

Comments

These statements reflect some of the attitudes which can create barriers to successful intercultural communication.

1 Business people do share certain beliefs and values, but it is highly misleading to believe that they are always stronger than other types of cultural influence (for example, national culture). Even McDonalds, which tries to standardize its products, has to adapt them to local taste, for instance, by serving lamb rather than beefburgers in India. The pressure of globalization can also lead to the strengthening of local identities; in Europe, for instance, the growth of the European Union is arguably leading to the strengthening of regional identity (as in the case of Scotland). The idea that people from different cultures can be fused together is at the heart of the concept of the 'melting pot', which was widely believed in in the USA until the mid-20th century. It was succeeded by concepts of cultural pluralism, or the 'salad bowl', where individual elements retain their own identity.

2 This is an ETHNOCENTRIC approach, and is unlikely to lead to success in business. Many opportunities will be missed if this is taken into account. The example of the use of the English language in DaimlerChrysler (see p. 1) illustrates this.

3 This is a commonly used phrase, and is useful in that it stresses the importance of considering the culture of the host. In practice, culture is so deeply rooted that it is not possible to change one's original culture and take on a new one.

4 Clearly, care should always be taken with generalizations, but at times they are necessary, and they can be useful as long as allowance is made for individual differences.

5 Bad intercultural training can do this. Good training avoids stereotyping, and encourages trainees to change their view in the light of what they observe.
6 Although this is true, intercultural training can sensitize you to the sorts of factors that may be influencing communication.
7 Simple lists of dos and don'ts are of rather limited help in making communication successful. While they are appealing to the busy business person, really effective intercultural interaction requires more than a knowledge of a few basic facts.

Perception

Exercise 5

Look at the picture. What do you see in it?

Comments

The picture, known as Rubin's vase, is a very famous example of how PERCEPTION works. It can be seen as a vase, or as two heads opposite each other. Most people can't see both at the same time, so some see the vase first, and some the heads. The fact that people perceive the same thing in different ways is particularly important in intercultural communication. The way we perceive is culturally determined, and the general lack of awareness of this is another barrier to intercultural communication.

Stereotypes

A stereotype is a fixed idea or image that many people have of a particular type of person or thing, but which is not true in reality. The word comes from printing, where it was used to describe the printing plate used to produce the same image over and over again.

Generalizations and categories are necessary, but when they are too rigid they can be a barrier to the effective interpretation of a situation. In intercultural communication, in particular, it is vital to distinguish between what is part of a person's cultural background and what is part of their personality.

In Figure 1.3, Hofstede uses the model of the pyramid to illustrate 'three levels of uniqueness in human mental programming'. Every person is in some way like all other people, some, or none.

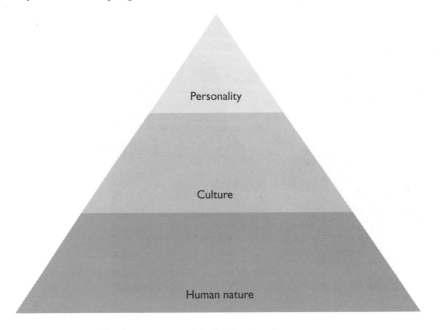

Figure 1.3: Levels of uniqueness (Hofstede 1991)

We do and think some things because we are humans: for instance, we want to sleep, eat, and survive. These are universal and inherited characteristics. We also do and think some things because of our culture: this might determine, for instance, when we eat and sleep, and how far we try to survive. These are characteristics which are specific to a particular group of people, and are learnt. We also do and think some things because of our individual personality. These characteristics are specific to us as individuals, and are both inherited and learnt. When trying to understand the behaviour of a person it is important to consider all of these three levels.

Within a culture there will be a range of attitudes, beliefs, values, and behaviour. It is possible to generalize about a culture, but care should be taken in applying those generalizations to individuals. When we meet an individual we can't tell where they are on the range (see Figure 1.4).

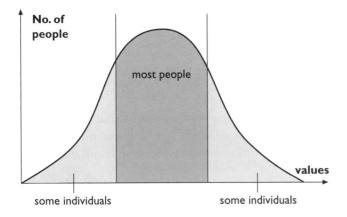

Figure 1.4: How attitudes and beliefs are distributed

Exercise 6

Look at the postcard 'The perfect European' and comment on the stereotypes.

Jonathan Swift wrote in 1725:

'I have ever hated all nations, professions and communities, and all my love is towards individuals . . . But principally, I hate and detest that animal called Man, although I heartily love John, Peter, Thomas and so forth.'

Interpretation

What is the communication problem here?

Exercise 7

A Japanese businessman is negotiating with a Norwegian partner. The Japanese says that the deal will be very difficult. The Norwegian asks how her company can help to solve the problems. The Japanese is puzzled by the question.

(Adapted from Adler 1997: 70)

Suggested answer

For the Japanese, the message was quite clear. For him, the statement that it would be difficult meant that there would be no deal. He expressed this INDIRECTLY, to be polite, and to avoid 'loss of FACE'. The Norwegian, not being aware of this, thought that there were some problems that could be resolved.

This is a case of misinterpretation, in which the two people have interpreted the same statement in completely different ways.

Gudykunst (1994: 129–36) suggests three ways of checking our interpretation of other people's behaviour.

1 *Perception checking*
  The aim of perception checking is to ensure that our interpretation of the other person's behaviour is what he or she meant it to be. First we have to describe what we thought the other person meant, before asking if this interpretation is correct. Even this process is culturally determined, and for people from some cultures could be too direct. 'If you are an INDIVIDUALIST communicating with a COLLECTIVIST, it is important to keep in mind that collectivists may not feel comfortable answering direct questions. In this case you may have to ask your perception checking questions more indirectly.'

2 *Listening effectively*
  It is important to distinguish between hearing (the physical process) and listening, which involves much more attention, and includes absorbing new information, checking it with what you already know, categorizing it, selecting ideas, and predicting what is coming next. Active listening involves showing the speaker that we are involved in the conversation, trying

to understand, and to understand them better (by asking questions, for instance, or restating what they have said).

3 *Giving feedback*
This is the verbal or non-verbal response to others. Again, the ways feedback is given vary widely across cultures, but it is often useful to follow the following guidelines:

- Be specific.
- Separate the feedback from the person.
- Present the problem as a mutual one.
- Mix negative with positive feedback.
- Provide feedback at an appropriate time.
- Use 'I' statements wherever possible.

Culture shock

Oberg described CULTURE SHOCK as follows:

> Culture shock is precipitated by the anxiety that results from losing all our familiar signs and symbols of social intercourse. These signs or cues include the thousand and one ways in which we orient ourselves to the situations of daily life: when to shake hands and what to say when we meet people, when and how to give tips, how to give orders to servants, how to make purchases, when to accept and when to refuse invitations, when to take statements seriously, and when not. Now these cues, which may be words, gestures, facial expressions, customs, or norms, are acquired by all of us in the course of growing up, and are as much a part of our culture as the language we speak, or the beliefs we accept. All of us depend for our peace of mind and our efficiency on hundreds of these cues, even though we are often not consciously aware of them.

> Some of the symptoms of culture shock are: excessive washing of the hands; excessive concern over drinking water, food, dishes, and bedding; fear of physical contact with attendants or servants; the absent, far-away stare (sometimes called 'the tropical stare'); a feeling of helplessness and a desire for dependence on long-term residents of one's own nationality; fits of anger over delays, and other minor frustrations; delay and outright refusal to learn the language of the host country; excessive fear of being cheated, robbed, and injured; excessive concern over minor pains and eruptions of the skin; and, finally, that terrible longing to be back home, to be able to have a good cup of coffee and a piece of apple pie, to walk into that corner drugstore, to visit one's relatives, and in general, to talk to people who really make sense.
>
> (Oberg 1960: 176, quoted in Furnham and Bochner 1986: 48)

Culture shock, 'transition shock', or 'the experience of foreignness' (Marx 1999) are the reactions to living in a new culture. 'Shock' is perhaps the wrong word, because the process can also be gradual. The symptoms of culture shock can include:

- strain
- sense of loss
- feeling rejected
- confusion
- anxiety
- helplessness
- obsession with hygiene.

Physical symptoms can include:

- headaches
- sleeplessness
- overeating
- desire for comfort foods (for example, chocolate)
- excessive consumption of alcohol
- stomach pains.

In Figure 1.5 Marx identifies various phases of culture shock.

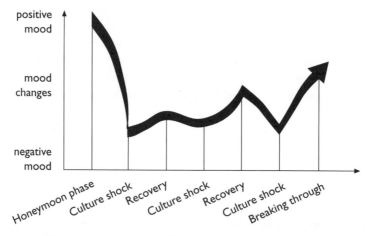

Figure 1.5: Phases of culture shock (Marx 1999)

To start with, everything is new and exciting; this is the 'honeymoon period'. Then, after a period of negative feelings, comes recovery. This can happen over a period of 3–6 months or longer, depending on the individual's personality and cultural distance. This cycle is repeated, and hopefully overcome, in the 'breaking through' phase.

Reverse culture shock, or 're-entry' shock, can be experienced on returning to your original culture. As Michael Paige pointed out, 'Culture shock is the expected confrontation with the unfamiliar. Re-entry shock is the unexpected confrontation with the familiar.' This can be more difficult than, say, the culture shock of going abroad. After the positive feelings of being back can come a feeling of alienation, connected with the realization that things have changed since you departed. There follows a period of adjustment, and of 'breaking through'.

How far you experience culture shock will depend on a number of factors, including your personality, how different the culture is from your own, the social support you receive, and the purpose of your stay.

Dealing with difference

Successful international managers

Exercise 8

Use the following statements to reflect on how well suited you are to be an international manager. How many are true of you?

1 I am a sociable person and have a lot of friends.
2 I enjoy travel, and learning about new cultures.
3 I have always been good at learning languages.
4 I enjoy dealing with ambiguous situations.
5 I am tolerant of people who disagree with me.
6 I am prepared to change plans according to what happens.
7 I am a good listener.
8 I can cope with stress.
9 I have experience of working abroad.
10 I have a partner/family who is/are also keen on living abroad.
11 I am patient when things don't work out as I want them too.
12 I prefer to work in a team rather than on my own.

The more of these statements you can honestly agree with, the more suitable you are for work in an international context.

Marx's research into what personnel managers in German companies looked for in international managers produced the following list, in order of priority:

- social competence
- openness to other ways of thinking
- cultural adaptation
- professional excellence
- language skills
- flexibility
- ability to manage/work in a team
- self-reliance/independence
- mobility
- ability to deal with stress
- adaptability of the family
- patience
- sensitivity.

(Marx 1999: 15)

Note that professional excellence doesn't come at the top of the list. Some companies have made the mistake of using technical skills as the only criterion for sending managers abroad; the results are rarely successful. Where aggression, speed, and competitiveness may be important in a monocultural environment, they could be dangerous in an intercultural one, where other qualities, such as adaptability, and a high tolerance for ambiguity, are more important.

It is also important to consider the family of the manager going abroad. Many foreign assignments fail because the partner or family is unhappy. The manager may be enjoying the challenges of an interesting new job and have the support of the colleagues at work, but the partner at home may feel isolated, especially if they have given up their career. If the children don't make friends, or are unhappy at school, this, too, will inevitably cause considerable tensions for all members of the family.

Cultural learning

Figure 1.6 shows different phases of cultural learning.

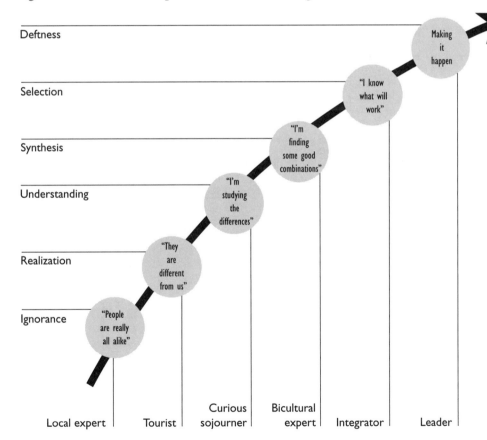

Figure 1.6: Phases of cultural learning (Clackworthy, personal communication)

At the lowest level is the belief that all people are alike. Then comes a recognition that there are differences, an acceptance of the differences, seeing ways of synthesizing the different ways, selecting, and making things run smoothly.

The process of cultural learning can be helped along by experience, reflection, and training. Intercultural training not only provides information but also develops skills, and encourages attitudes to enable people to progress along the cultural learning curve. The model of the Johari Window, developed by the Americans Joseph Luft and Harrington Ingram, can be adapted to illustrate what successful cultural learning is. The name comes from a combination of their names (Jo and Hari).

In Handy's adaptation of the model in Figure 1.7 there is a house with four rooms. Room 1 is the area which we are aware of, and where we share common beliefs, attitudes, values, and behaviour with others. While others can see into Room 2, we can't. We can see into Room 4, but others can't. Room 3 is hidden to both of us. The challenge is to extend the area which we can both see into (Room 1), to increase understanding of ourselves and each other.

Figure 1.7: Johari window (Hornday 1990: 63)

A further model of cultural learning has been developed by Hoecklin (see Figure 1.8).

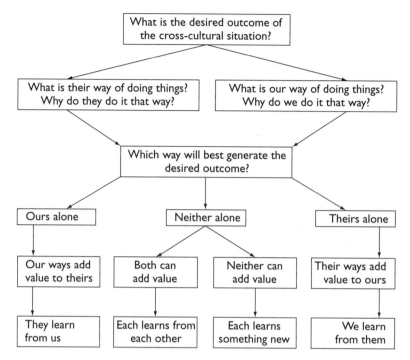

Figure 1.8: A model of cultural learning (Hoecklin 1994)

Managing diversity

Exercise 9

The following case is set in the UK. What would you advise Sally to do?

Over a period of about five years Sally, who is a manager within a private sector organization, has seen her team change in cultural composition. From what was once a white team, staffed predominantly by white staff, the team now includes four black staff, out of a total of 15 people.

The black staff participate in team meetings, but they are not heard equally. For example, on a number of occasions their suggestions have been ignored.

A few incidents have occurred. Some 'lighthearted' jokes have been directed at one of the black staff about what they have brought in for their lunch, and comments made about the smell of the food; some of the language used by white colleagues has been subtly, and sometimes not so subtly, objected to by black staff. The use of the term 'coloured' about clients raised the black staff's objection that the term 'coloured' had been imposed on them in the past, defining them in a subordinate and oppressive relationship. They also pointed out that black people have now adopted the term 'black', thereby asserting the element of choice born of independent status. The white staff's view was that the black staff were being 'over-sensitive', and that the objections which have been made to the use of language should not be taken seriously. The behaviour of the white staff remained unchanged.

Two black members of the staff approached the manager and asked if a black workers' group could be set up.

(Ansari and Jackson 1995: 89–91)

Suggested answer
The manager needs to take some action. The formation of the group would provide the black workers with a forum where they could meet, and her support for it would send a signal to the white workers. The danger of forming the group is that the communication between the groups might polarize, and get even worse.

Further action might include:

- Getting feedback from the white workers to find out why they are behaving as they are.
- Making sure that all the staff understand the reasons for the formation of the group.
- Encouraging staff to challenge discriminatory remarks or actions.
- Offering training to all staff.

Exercise 10

Many companies now have a diversity policy. One example is Procter and Gamble (see page 6). The text below is taken from their statement on diversity.

Compare the Procter and Gamble policy with that of other companies that you are familiar with.

> Our intent is to develop all employees to their full potential. To achieve this goal, we have human resource systems in place that support individual development, and we regularly review those systems to make sure they work well for everyone, including women and the various population groups that make up our minority workforce.
>
> Ongoing support systems we have in place include:
>
> - Career discussions, performance appraisals, assignment plans, transfer and promotion plans.
> - Grass roots/informal network support groups which have existed at different sites for a number of years.
> - Mentoring to provide informal support and guidance, in addition to the coaching and training provided by each employee's direct manager.
>
> (Procter and Gamble)

Further reading

Cultural learning

One guide to coping with living in a different culture, enriched with a variety of extracts from literature, is:

Storti, C. 1990. *The Art of Crossing Cultures*. Yarmouth: Intercultural Press.

Managing diversity

A practical guide to managing diversity is:

Ansari, K. H. and J. Jackson. 1995. *Managing Cultural Diversity at Work*. London: Kogan Page.

2 CULTURAL DIMENSIONS

Survey of research

Intercultural communication is a relatively new field of research. It is also interdisciplinary, and so draws on many different areas of investigation. Some of them are shown in Figure 2.1.

Many of the following ideas come from the USA, where companies were faced with the challenge of finding ways to help people of many different cultural origins to live and work together. After the Second World War there was a realization in business that the USA needed to know more about other cultures if it was to increase its overseas trade. Input also came from the US army, which had been operating in many different countries, and faced numerous intercultural problems.

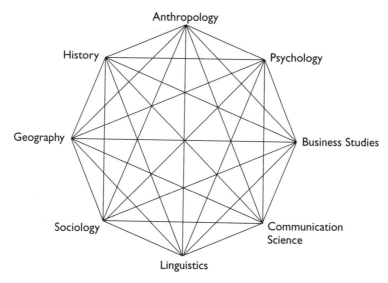

Figure 2.1: Disciplines involved in intercultural communication

Hall

Some of the first research was done by Edward Hall, the anthropologist who trained government employees in the US Foreign Service Institute during the 1950s. He became well-known for his books, such as *The Silent Language* (1959) and *The Hidden Dimension* (1966). He is particularly famous for his work on low- and high-context cultures, and on different concepts of time. His books are easy to read, and still very popular today.

Kluckhohn and Strodtbeck

Research conducted by two anthropologists, Florence Kluckhohn and Fred Strodtbeck (1961), identified five key orientations of basic importance to human beings, and found that within each orientation there is a range of beliefs and values. Their work has been the basis of much further work in the area.

1 Human nature

At one extreme there are those who think that humans are basically evil, and cannot be trusted. In the middle are people who think there are both good and bad people in the world. At the other extreme are those who see humans as basically good.

2 Man–nature relationship

At one extreme there is the belief that life is determined by external forces, such as God, fate, or nature. In the middle range are those who believe that man should live in harmony with nature. At the other extreme are those who believe that man can control nature.

3 Time sense

This ranges from a tradition-bound, past-orientated view of the world, to a present orientation ('living for the moment'), to a goal-orientated future orientation.

4 Activity

At one extreme there are those who think it is enough to just 'be'. In the middle are those who look for inner development, and at the other extreme there is action orientation, with a belief in working for rewards.

5 Social relations

These range from a belief that there are natural leaders and natural followers, to an orientation towards collective decisions, to individualism, and a belief in equal rights.

Hofstede

Geert Hofstede, the Dutch social psychologist and engineer, collected data from employees of IBM in the late 1960s and early 1970s. His database covered employees working in 72 of the company's national subsidiaries, who followed 38 different occupations, and spoke 20 languages. More than 116,000 questionnaires were distributed, each with over 100 questions. Hofstede published his findings in 1980 in a groundbreaking book called *Culture's Consequences*, which has had an enormous influence on the further development of the field. He identified four dimensions:

1 INDIVIDUALISM/COLLECTIVISM
2 UNCERTAINTY AVOIDANCE
3 POWER DISTANCE
4 MASCULINITY/FEMININITY.

Hofstede later extended his work to include a fifth dimension: LONG-TERM ORIENTATION. Although generally highly respected, his work has been criticized for concentrating too much on national cultures.

Trompenaars

Another Dutchman, Fons Trompenaars, carried out research on 15,000 managers from 28 countries. His findings can be found in the very successful book, *Riding the Waves of Culture* (Trompenaars and Hampden-Turner 1997). He describes three main cultural dimensions:

1 relationships with people
2 attitudes to time
3 attitudes to the environment.

There are eight further sub-categories. Trompenaars builds on previous research to extend the range of cultural dimensions.

Trompenaars has done a great deal to make the problems of intercultural communication known to a wider audience, although the validity of some of his approach and findings has been questioned by some other researchers, including Hofstede.

Non-verbal communication

This section gives examples of some areas of non-verbal communication which can differ between cultures.

Body language (kinesics)

This includes body movement, body position, and facial expressions, as well as dress.

Figure 2.2: Gestures (Axtell 1991)

Exercise 11

Look at the pictures in Figure 2.2, and say what each of the gestures means to you.

Suggested answer
The same gesture can mean different things to people from different cultures, as shown in the following examples.

1 In the USA, this means 'A-OK', in France, 'zero', in Japan, 'money', and in Tunisia, 'I'll kill you.'
2 In Germany, this means 'two', or victory; in Britain, it means 'victory' if the palm of the hand is facing outwards, but is a rude gesture if the palm is facing inwards.
3 In Greece and Italy, this means 'goodbye', in the USA, it means 'come here'.
4 In many cultures, this means that everything is fine. In Nigeria and Australia, it is a rude gesture.

Even the way people dress for business differs widely across cultures. One famous example is that of a businessman from continental Europe, wearing a sports jacket and tie, arriving for a meeting in London with his British counterpart wearing a suit, to be greeted with the words, 'Did the airline lose your luggage?' To the British partner, the other man's choice of a sports jacket suggested inappropriate informality. As always, it is not only national cultural differences that are important; corporate culture can differ widely, too, even within the same industry: a Microsoft executive, for example, might be dressed very differently from someone employed by IBM.

Critical incident 1

What do you think is happening here?

> Sales representatives from Germany and Britain are in a difficult negotiation. Things are getting tense. Franz Bauer sits upright and is disturbed as Jim Banks relaxes in his chair. Franz Bauer feels that Jim is not taking the negotiation seriously. Jim feels that Herr Bauer is getting more and more aggressive.

Comments

The German's upright position indicates the seriousness with which he is taking the situation, while Jim's posture in the chair indicates his wish to defuse the situation. The two people misinterpret each other's behaviour, and so the situation escalates. In some cultures travellers should be careful to avoid exposing certain parts of their body. In some Arab cultures, for example, the sole of the foot is considered dirty, and should never be shown, so anyone who adopts the local custom of sitting on the floor, for instance, has to take care to avoid doing this.

Eye contact (oculistics)

Critical incident 2

What do you think is happening here?

1 A British expatriate living in Germany complains about being stared at in the underground train. 'They stare at me straight in the face as if I've come from another planet', he said.
2 A US manager reports problems with Japanese staff. 'I asked them how the project was going and, of course, not much has been done. I was suspicious when they didn't even look me in the eye', he said.

Comments

The length of time that it is acceptable to look directly at someone can also differ from one country to the next. In some cultures, looking someone in the eye is taken as a sign of interest and honesty. In others, however, this can be seen as a sign of disrespect. Visitors gradually learn not to look too directly at the person they are talking to, in case they are thought to be staring intrusively.

Touch (haptics)

Critical incident 3
What do you think is happening here?

> A European manager who came to work in the US subsidiary of an insurance company was pleased to find that he had an excellent secretary. After she had completed yet another piece of work long before the deadline, he went up to her, tapped her on the shoulder, and said, 'Pat, thanks again. It really is such a help that you are here.' Her response was to complain to the manager's boss.

Comments

Where, how, and how often people touch each other varies widely across cultures. Even in the business world there are large variations. In the USA, the actions of some male employees in touching female employees, whether innocently or otherwise, has given rise to law suits for sexual harassment.

When and how often people shake hands varies widely, too. A group of British investment bankers felt that their German colleagues shook hands excessively, and advised a British colleague going to a meeting in Germany that they should 'shake hands with anything that moves'. In other cultures, hugging or kissing are more appropriate forms of greeting, even in a business context.

Body distance (proxemics)

Critical incident 4
What do you think is happening here?

> Julio, an Argentinian student who is keen to improve his English, is attending a course in Business English. He often stays behind after the class to ask the British lecturer, Jim Ford, some questions. When Julio approaches, Mr Ford looks uneasy and begins to move away. Julio wonders whether Mr Ford doesn't like him, if he is asking too many questions, or whether students are not supposed to ask questions after class.

Comments

How close you get to another person when talking to them differs widely across cultures. Research has shown that in the USA the 'comfort zone' is about an arm's length. In Latin America, the tendency is for people to get closer to each other than people, for instance, in the UK. The fact that this is a tendency doesn't, of course, mean that all British people do this. Julio's explanations of Mr Ford's behaviour might be correct, but it could also be that the lecturer feels uneasy because the student is coming too close to him.

Paralanguage

It is not only words used that convey a message, but also a range of other factors, such as our tone of voice, and the speed or pitch of what we say.

Critical incident 5
What do you think is happening here?

A British–Polish joint venture is running into problems. Magda Sapinska, one of the key members of the Polish sales staff, has been sent to London to work with the UK partner company. The London office is very impressed with her performance, and would like her to stay on for another six months. Geoff Woodside, the British manager of the London office, asks her to ring Warsaw to see what they think. The telephone conversation is in Polish. Although Geoff can't speak Polish, it quickly seems clear to him that Magda is having a row with the Warsaw office. When she puts the phone down, he says to her, 'Magda, sorry to have got you into this mess— I hope we haven't made you unpopular in Warsaw.' Magda is puzzled and says, 'What are you talking about? Everything's fine—Warsaw has given us the OK.'

Comments
Intonation patterns and tone of voice vary widely in different cultures. What in one culture sounds like a hysterical argument, in another would be considered to be the norm for a reasonable discussion. Geoff Woodside came to the wrong conclusion about the tone of the conversation when he judged the sound of people speaking in Polish by the very different intonation patterns in English.

Trompenaars provides a useful diagram to illustrate some possible patterns (see Figure 2.3).

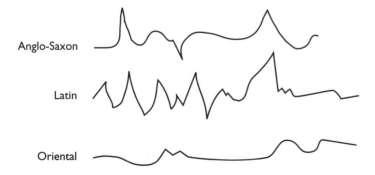

Figure 2.3: Intonation patterns (Trompenaars and Hampden-Turner 1997)

Turn-taking

Critical incident 6
What do you think is happening here?

> Researchers looking into intercultural communication asked an Italian and a Japanese businessman to find out particular information from each other. They interviewed them separately after the conversation. The Italian said 'He seemed like a nice enough guy, but he never really said anything'; the Japanese said 'He was very friendly, but he never gave me a chance to speak.'

Comments
The way that turn-taking works in a conversation, and the role of silence, also differ between cultures. In some it is acceptable, and even desirable to interrupt, whereas in some others it is normal to wait for your partner to finish speaking before making your point. In some other cultures, a period of silence between contributions is accepted as the norm.

Trompenaars illustrates this in Figure 2.4.

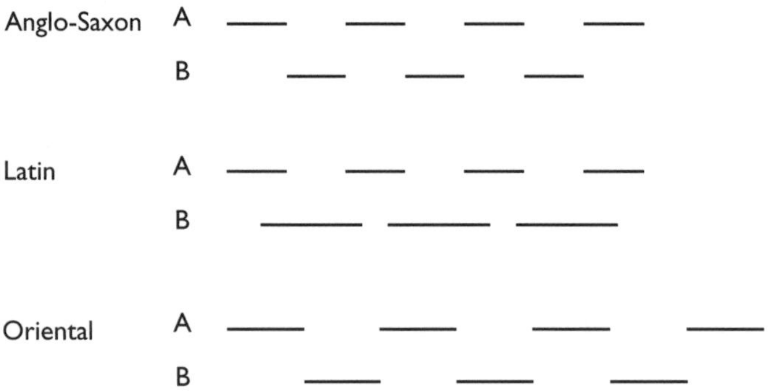

Figure 2.4: Turn-taking (Trompenaars and Hampden-Turner 1997)

Communication style

Context

Critical incident 7
What do you think is happening here?

> The US marketing manager of a major car producer was finding it increasingly difficult to work in Japan. In meetings, the Japanese colleagues hardly ever said anything. When they were asked if they agreed to his suggestions

they always said 'Yes', but they didn't do anything to follow up the ideas. The only time they opened up was in a bar in the evening, but that was getting stressful, as they seemed to expect him to go out with them on a regular basis.

Comments

This illustrates what Hall called LOW- and HIGH-CONTEXT CULTURES. 'A high-context (HC) communication or message is one in which most of the information is either in the physical context or internalized in the person, while very little is in the coded, explicit, transmitted part of the message. A low-context (LC) communication is just the opposite, i.e. the mass of information is vested in the explicit code' (Hall 1976: 91).

In high-context cultures, such as Japan, meaning does not always have to be put into words. Non-verbal clues are important, as is the context in which the situation takes place. Even the meaning of words can depend on the context. For example, 'yes' can mean anything from 'I agree', to 'I am listening', to 'no'. Relationship building is important in high-context cultures, and there is an emphasis on getting to know one's business partner. In low-context cultures (such as the USA) meaning is made explicit, and put into words. These cultures tend to be task-centred rather than relationship-centred.

Figure 2.5 shows Hall's concept, and a possible positioning of some national cultures on the scale from low to high context.

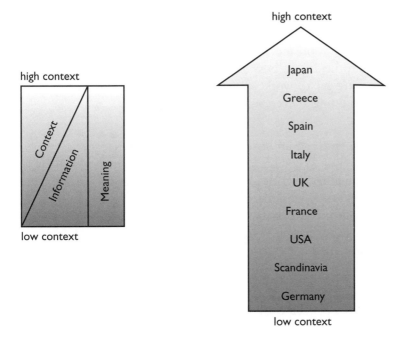

Figure 2.5: Low and high context (Hall 1976)

Trompenaars relates this to what he calls 'circling around or getting to the point'. In high-context cultures people start from the general and then get down to the specifics, while in low-context cultures it is the other way round, i.e. starting with the specifics and then going to the general (see Figure 2.6).

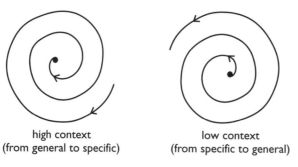

high context
(from general to specific)

low context
(from specific to general)

Figure 2.6: Low and high context (Trompenaars and Hampden-Turner 1997)

Directness

Critical incident 8

What do you think is happening here?

A Belgian manager working in Thailand is unhappy that his secretary regularly arrives at work at least 30 minutes, and sometimes as much as one hour, late for work. He knows that the traffic in Bangkok is bad, but this is getting ridiculous. One morning, when she arrives late again, he explodes in front of the others in the busy office. He then takes her aside and tells her that if she can't get to work on time she may risk losing her job. She responds by handing in her resignation.

Comments

The manager has made a number of mistakes, by not understanding that in some cultures it is not acceptable to criticize people in front of others. This is because a public telling-off leads to a 'loss of face'. It can also be unacceptable to show emotion at the workplace. Although there are always going to be times when criticism is necessary, in this cultural context, direct criticism, even in a one-to-one situation, is not acceptable. Verluyten, who has carried out research into INDIRECTNESS and conflict avoidance amongst executives in a range of countries, suggests that there are three ways of dealing with the situation:

1 Blur the SENDER. This means that you don't criticize the person directly, but do so through a friend or colleague.
2 Blur the receiver. This means that you mention the problem in front of the whole group, rather than picking out an individual.

3 Blur the message. This could mean talking about a hypothetical case, or asking indirect questions, such as 'Do you still live out of town?' or 'How is the baby?' It might even involve giving excessive praise—the secretary would then know that something was wrong.

(Verluyten 1999)

Exercise 12

Sometimes the language used can be seen as too direct.

Put the suggested phrases in the order 'most direct' to 'most indirect'. You want someone to open the window:

1 Would you be so kind as to open the window?
2 It's hot in here.
3 Please open the window.
4 Open the window.
5 Could you possibly open the window?
6 I was wondering if you could open the window.
7 Would you like to open the window?
8 Don't you think it's a little hot in here?

Suggested answer
A possible order would be 4, 3, 6, 5, 7, 1, 2, 8, although a lot depends on the intonation used. Some of the longer phrases could sound very sarcastic, while some of the shorter ones can be extremely polite.

Exercise 13

Try to make the following more polite:

1 You must do this by Monday.
2 Your report contained a lot of mistakes.
3 Give me two beers. (ordering beers at the bar)
4 You forgot the sales figures.

Suggested answers
1 We need this by Monday.
2 There seem to be a lot of mistakes in the report.
3 Could I have two beers please?
4 I can't find the sales figures.

In the above examples, politeness is brought about by removing the receiver from the statements by stressing either the message or the sender.

In the English-speaking world, there are wide variations in how far this indirectness is seen as necessary. Lewis, in his book *When Cultures Collide* (1996), suggests some different ways in which American and British business people might express the same thing. Here are some examples:

USA   Jack'll blow his top.
GB   Our chairman might tend to disagree.

USA   You're talking rubbish.
GB   I'm not quite with you on that.

USA   You gotta be kidding.
GB   Hm, that's an interesting idea.

USA   I tell you, I can walk away from this deal.
GB   We'll have to do our homework.

(Lewis 1996: 171)

Person and task

Critical incident 9

What do you think is happening here?

A group of German academics were meeting for a Friday afternoon seminar.
A paper was presented, after which there was a heated discussion. An American
guest professor was disturbed by the atmosphere, and had the impression that
the professors didn't like each other at all. She was surprised that after the
discussion had ended they all left the room in a good mood, wishing each other
a good weekend.

Comments

The German professors were focused on the task at hand (i.e. the discussion
of the academic paper), while the US colleague was concentrating on the
relationship between the people present—and misinterpreted the tone of
heated discussion as meaning that the people didn't like each other.

In many cultures, it is more important to preserve a relationship than to get
the task done. Jobs, for instance, may be given to family and friends, rather
than to the person with the best qualifications. Figure 2.7 shows the interface
between the task at hand, the individuals, and the team.

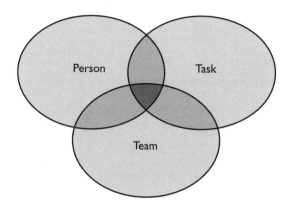

Figure 2.7: Person and task

Time (chronemics)

Polychronic and monochronic

Critical incident 10

What do you think is happening here?

> A British businessman in Saudi Arabia is keen to secure an important deal. He has a tight schedule, and can't afford to waste any time. His frustration increases because he has to wait for ages to get an appointment with his Saudi partner. Meetings never start on time, and when they do, there are frequent interruptions, with people coming in to get papers signed. The Saudi partner even takes phone calls when his visitor is in the room.

Comments

This is a classic example of the difference between what Hall calls POLY-CHRONIC and MONOCHRONIC cultures. In polychronic cultures, it is acceptable to do several things at the same time, and the approach to deadlines is flexible. In monochronic cultures, one thing is done at a time, with great stress being laid on meeting deadlines and schedules.

Linear, cyclical, and event-related

Critical incident 11
What do you think is happening here?

It was a bright sunny morning, not too hot, near Kuala Lumpur, the capital of Malaysia. While the British visitor was slowly getting ready to go out, he watched the lizards as they scurried across the bedroom wall. How could they get in and out of such tiny cracks? To his English mind, there was plenty of time to take a leisurely shower and organize his papers, since the car to take him to the meeting was not due until 10 o'clock. However, he was just pulling on his trousers when there was a knock at the door. Hastily finishing dressing, he opened it.

'Shall we get going?' said the driver. It was just half-past eight.

'But weren't we starting at ten?'

'Yes, but it's a lovely morning!'
(Adapted from Hickson and Pugh 1995: 41)

Comments
This reflects different attitudes to time. In Malaysia, time is flexible. Sometimes this means that appointments take place after the agreed time, but it can also mean that they take place earlier. This is known as 'rubber time', referring back to the times of the rubber tree plantations introduced during British colonial rule.

Linear concept of time
This concept, as found, for instance, in the USA, sees time as a line which can be broken up into segments.

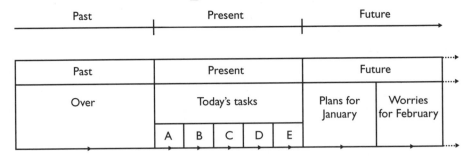

Figure 2.8: Concept of time (Lewis 1996)

It passes from the past to the future and can be saved, spent, wasted, or lost. It is the product of an industrial society which required the precise measurement of time, planning, and discipline.

Cyclical concept of time

This concept is inspired by the daily and yearly routines of agricultural life, in which time is not seen as a scarce resource, because it keeps coming all the time. It is taken for granted that people should adapt to natural cycles.

Event-related concept of time

According to this concept, time is when something happens. 'When something happens, for instance when the roof starts leaking, one takes action, and not before, even if one is aware of the damage to the roof. The event, such as the leak in the roof, triggers the action: the repair. It is not a result of conscious planning, rather a result of a happening.' (Dahl 1994: 80). Time cannot be wasted or saved. The bus does not leave when a timetable says it should, but when it is full.

Past, present, and future

The attitude to past, present, and future differs widely between cultures. Some put more emphasis on the past, while others stress the present, and others again think in the long term. In his 1991 book (see Recommended Reading), Hofstede listed 23 countries in an index of long-term orientation.

Cultures with SHORT-TERM ORIENTATION tend to have the following features:

- respect for traditions
- people prepared to overspend to keep up with their neighbours
- small amount of savings
- people expect quick results.

Cultures with LONG-TERM ORIENTATION tend to have the following features:

- traditions adapted for modern context
- people thrifty
- large amount of savings
- people persevere for slow results.

(Adapted from Hofstede 1991: 173)

When Russian managers reported on why so many joint ventures with Western companies failed, they said that one factor was that their Western partners showed a lack of interest in their country's history. This is illustrated in research into how people see the relationship between the past, the present, and the future. Using Cottle circle test, people were asked to draw three circles to illustrate the relationship between the past, the present, and the future. Some of the results are shown in Figure 2.9.

This suggests that in the USA, for example, the future is more important for people than the past, whereas in Russia the importance of past and future are more equally balanced.

For many cultures the past is visualized as being behind us, and the future in front of us. However, this concept is by no means universal, as is shown in Figure 2.10. In Madagascar, for example, the past is seen as in front of us (we can see what has already happened) and the future is behind us (we can't see it yet).

Space

Just as body distance can vary between cultures, so can the perception of space.

Critical incident 12

What do you think is happening here?

> A German guest professor in the USA, who always kept his office door closed, was surprised that very few students came to see him for advice—his American colleagues seemed to be more popular. He wondered if the Americans rejected him because he was German. He was especially irritated one day when he found that the students had stuck a sign on the door saying 'Beware of the dog'.

Comments

Many universities in the USA have an 'open door' policy—the office door is only closed when a private meeting is taking place. The American students interpreted the closed door of the German professor as a sign of his unfriendliness.

Even the way offices are laid out indicates different attitudes to space. Figure 2.11 shows typical office plans in Japan and the USA.

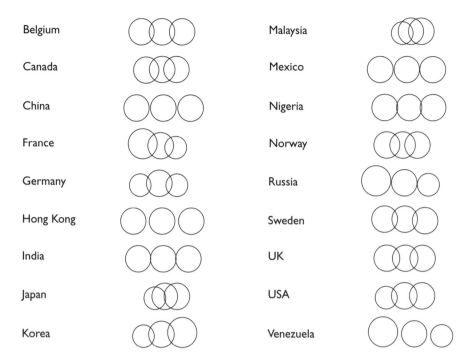

Belgium		Malaysia	
Canada		Mexico	
China		Nigeria	
France		Norway	
Germany		Russia	
Hong Kong		Sweden	
India		UK	
Japan		USA	
Korea		Venezuela	

Figure 2.9: Cottle circle test (Trompenaars and Hampden-Turner 1997)

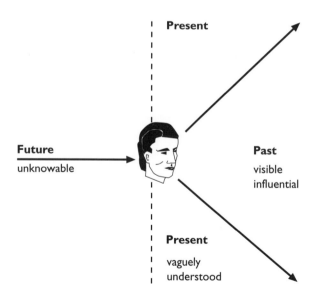

Figure 2.10: Visualization of time (Lewis 1996)

Typical Japanese Office Space

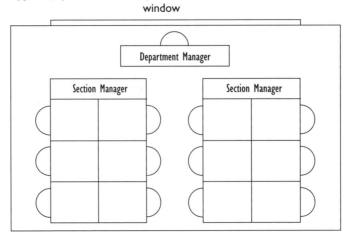

Typical American Office Space

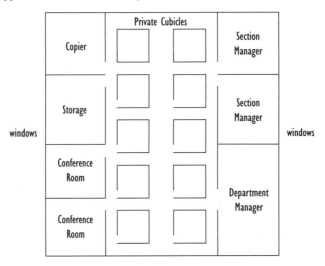

Figure 2.11: Office space (Brake et al. 1995)

Power

Critical incident 13

What do you think is happening here?

> A British employee of a German state institute attached to a government ministry was frustrated at the time it took for decisions to be made. To speed things up, he faxed documents directly to his counterpart at the ministry. When the head of department at the institute found this out, he was extremely annoyed, and demanded that he should see every fax before it was sent to the ministry.

For the British employee, the important thing was to get the job done, whereas for the German, respect for the company hierarchy, and the importance of following official channels of communication, were of utmost importance.

Differing attitudes to hierarchy and the distribution of power have been illustrated in research done by Laurent and Hofstede. Laurent (1983) suggested that: 'In order to have efficient work relationships, it is often necessary to bypass the hierarchical line.' Table 2.1 shows the varying levels of disagreement with this statement in different countries.

Percent disagreement across countries

Sweden	Great Britain	United States	Netherlands	France	Germany	Italy
22%	31%	32%	39%	42%	46%	75%

Table 2.1: Western conceptions of management (Laurent 1983)

Hofstede defined power distance as 'the extent to which the less powerful members of institutions and organizations within a country expect and accept that power is distributed unequally'.

According to Hofstede, in large power distance cultures, subordinates expect to be told what to do, and there is a wide range of salaries. In low-power distance cultures, by contrast, subordinates and superiors consider themselves as equals, hierarchies are flat, and salary ranges are relatively small.

Small power distance cultures tend to have the following features:

- people want to minimize inequality
- decentralization is popular
- there is a narrow range of salaries
- subordinates expect to be consulted
- the ideal boss is a democrat
- people disapprove of status.

Large power distance cultures tend to have the following features:

- inequalities are expected and welcomed
- centralization is popular
- there is a wide range of salaries
- the ideal boss is an autocrat
- privileges for managers are expected.

(Adapted from Hofstede 1991: 37)

Individual and group

Individualism

Critical incident 14

What do you think is happening here?

> An American manager working in Japan is particularly impressed by the performance of one member of his team. At the next team meeting he praises this person in front of the group. The rest of the Japanese team look uneasy.

Comments

Japan is seen to be a highly collectivist culture, in which decisions are made by the group rather than by individuals. The Japanese are uneasy because one of the group has been singled out for attention. A better approach would be for the US manager to praise the work of the whole team.

Individualist cultures stress self-realization, whereas collectivist ones require that the individual fits into the group. The collectivist idea is illustrated by the Japanese saying 'The nail that stands out must be hammered down'. In individualist cultures, people look after themselves and their immediate family, whereas in collectivist ones they look after a wider group, in exchange for loyalty.

Collectivist cultures tend to have the following features:

- identity is based on the social network to which you belong
- harmony should be maintained
- communication is high context
- employer–employee relationships are like a family link
- decisions on employing people take the group into account
- management is management of groups
- relationship is more important than task.

Individualist cultures tend to have the following features:

- identity is based on the individual
- honest people speak their mind
- communication is low context
- employer–employee relationships are based on a contract
- decisions to employ people takes skills into account
- management is management of individuals
- task is more important than relationship.

(Adapted from Hofstede 1991: 67)

Universalism and particularism

Exercise 14

Trompenaars asked people from a range of different countries what they thought about the following situation. Consider your own response, and then compare it with the results of the survey.

> You are riding in a car driven by a close friend. He hits a pedestrian. You know he was going at least 35 miles per hour in an area of the city where the speed limit is 20 miles per hour. There are no witnesses. His lawyer says that if you are prepared to testify under oath that he was only driving at that speed, it may save him from serious consequences.

> What right has your friend to expect you to protect him?

> 1a My friend has a definite right to expect me to testify to the lower figure.
> 1b He has some right as a friend to expect me to testify to the lower figure.
> 1c He has no right as a friend to expect me to testify to the lower figure.

> What do you think you would do in view of the obligations of a sworn witness and the obligation to your friend?

> 1d Testify that he was going 20 miles an hour.
> 1e Not testify that he was going 20 miles an hour.

(Trompenaars and Hampden-Turner 1997: 33–5)

Table 2.2 shows some extreme differences between Venezuela, where two-thirds of the people would be willing to lie to the police to protect their friend, and North America and Northern Europe, where the rules are considered to be more important than a relationship with a friend. Trompenaars calls these two groups PARTICULARISTS and UNIVERSALISTS. A universalist business person may say of a particularist partner that 'they cannot be trusted because they will always help their friends', whereas the particularist will say of the universalist that 'you cannot trust them; they would not even help their friends.'

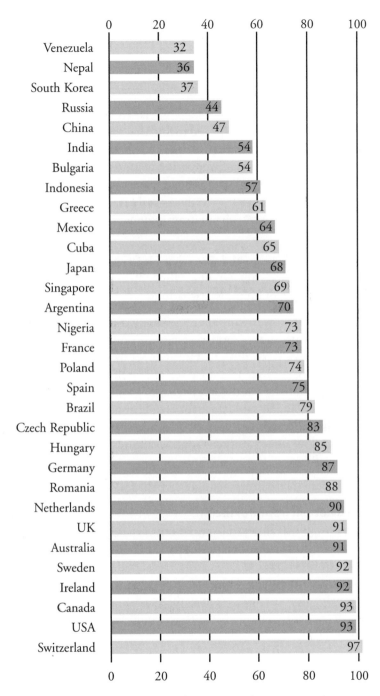

Table 2.2: Percentage of respondents opting for a universalist system rather than a particular social group (Trompenaars and Hampden-Turner 1997)

Uncertainty

Critical incident 15

What do you think is happening here?

> After taking over a British investment bank, German bankers in the corporate finance department were surprised to find that their British partners were earning considerably more than them, and that the team was frequently changing, since senior staff were being recruited, or 'poached', by rival banks. By contrast, most of the German team had been in the same bank since the beginning of their careers, and would not consider a change to a rival bank, even if they were offered more money.

Comments

This incident reflects different attitudes to what Hofstede calls 'uncertainty avoidance', which he suggests is 'the extent to which the members of a culture feel threatened by uncertain or unknown situations'.

Britain has a considerably lower score than Germany. The critical incident is an example of this, with more emphasis being put on career stability in Germany than in Britain. According to Hofstede, cultures with high uncertainty avoidance have 'a lower tolerance for ambiguity, which expresses itself in higher levels of anxiety and energy release, greater need for formal rules and absolute truth, and less tolerance for people or groups with deviant behaviour'. For high uncertainty avoidance cultures 'what is different is dangerous', while in low uncertainty avoidance cultures 'what is different is curious'.

Weak uncertainty avoidance cultures tend to have the following features:

- uncertainty is a normal feature of life
- people are comfortable in ambiguous situations
- there should not be more rules than necessary
- tolerance of innovative ideas
- motivation by achievement.

Strong uncertainty avoidance cultures tend to have the following features:

- uncertainty is a threat
- people fear ambiguous situations
- there is an emotional need for rules
- resistance to innovation
- motivation by security.

(Adapted from Hofstede 1991: 125)

Male and female

Critical incident 16

What do you think is happening here?

'As a young Dutch engineer I once applied for a junior management job with an American engineering company which had recently settled in Flanders, the Dutch-speaking part of Belgium. I felt well qualified: with a degree from the senior technical university of the country, good grades, a record of active participation in student associations, and three years' experience as an engineer with a well-known, although somewhat sleepy Dutch company. I had written a short letter indicating my interest and providing some data on my career to date. I was invited to appear in person, and after a long train ride I was soon facing the American plant manager. I behaved politely and modestly, as I knew an applicant should, and waited for the other man to ask the usual questions which would enable him to find out how qualified I was. To my surprise, he asked me very few of the questions I thought we should be discussing. Instead, he wanted me to give him some very detailed facts about my experience in tool design using English words I did not understand, and the relevance of which escaped me. Those were the things I could learn within a week once I worked there. After half an hour of uncomfortable misunderstandings, he said 'Sorry – we need a first class man.' And I was out in the street!'

(Hofstede 1991: 79)

Comments

The author explains the incident in the following way. For the American, the Dutch person undersold himself. The CV was too short and too modest, since he expected the interviewer to find out more about him in the interview, including questions about his outside activities. In contrast to Dutch applicants, American candidates tend to oversell themselves. Their CVs are full of superlatives and minute details of all their skills. They aim to show more assertiveness than Dutch applicants, and to promise more than they are likely to achieve in practice.

Hofstede explains this situation with the dimension he calls 'masculinity and femininity'. In masculine cultures, the roles of men and women are distinct, in that 'men are supposed to be assertive, tough, and focused on material success, whereas women are supposed to be more modest, tender, and concerned with the quality of life.' In feminine cultures, the roles of men and women overlap, (and) both men and women are supposed to be modest, tender, and concerned with the quality of life' (Hofstede 1991: 82–3).

According to Hofstede, feminine cultures tend to have the following features:

- caring for others is a dominant value
- relationships are important
- people should be modest
- both men and women deal with facts and feelings
- people work to live
- managers aim for consensus
- equality, solidarity, and quality are important at work
- conflicts are solved by compromise.

Masculine cultures tend to have the following features:

- material success is a dominant value
- things are important
- men are assertive
- women deal with feelings
- people live to work
- managers are expected to be decisive
- competition and performance are important at work
- conflicts are fought out.

(Adapted from Hofstede 1991: 96)

Nature

Brake, Walker, and Walker (1995) identify three attitudes to nature and the environment:

1 Control: people can dominate their environment; it can be changed to fit human needs.
2 Harmony: people should live in harmony with the world around them.
3 Constraint: people are constrained by the world around them. Fate, luck, and change all play a significant role.

Exercise 15

Match the statements below to the three categories (control, harmony, and constraint).

a Don't rock the boat.
b When the going gets tough, the tough get going.
c Go with the flow.
d Go for it.
e God willing.
f Life is what you make of it.
g It's all a matter of luck, really.

Suggested answer

Control b, d, f

Harmony a, c

Constraint e, g

Trompenaars asked the people in his survey if they thought it was worth trying to control nature. His results are shown in Table 2.4.

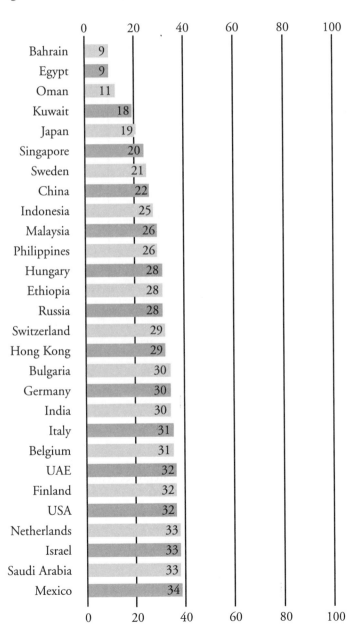

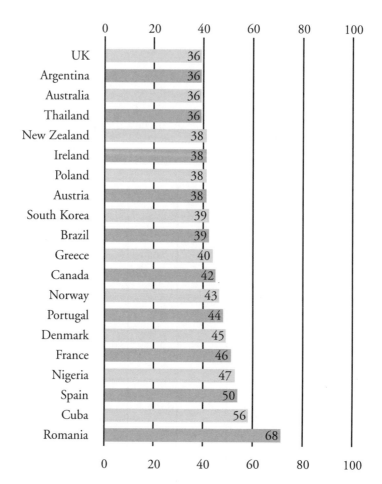

Figure 2.4: Percentage of people who think it is worth trying to control nature (Trompenaars and Hampden-Turner 1997)

3 BUSINESS COMMUNICATION

Managing people

A good manager

Exercise 16

What do you think are the qualities of a good manager?

Suggested answer
Very different answers to this question come from people from different cultures. In some cultures many people will value formal qualifications, while in others stress will be placed on interpersonal skills. A survey in Brazil showed that 'charisma' was seen as very important by many people. This helped some management trainers to understand why it was so difficult to sell their services: people thought that you were either born to manage other people or not, and that training would have very little effect.

Table 3.1 shows the results of research into how managers in an international computer hardware company saw the qualities of an effective manager.

How do you assess the general effectiveness of a manager?

	GB	USA	D	F
Ability to take decisions	□	□	✗	▨
Clear tracking of projects and process	□	▨	■	□
Effective use of resources	□	□	✗	■
Good result/achieving goals	✗	■	■	□
Is respected and people want to work for him or her	■	□	▨	□
Creating a good working relationship	■	▨	■	□

□ Not mentioned   ✗ 1–19% mentioned
▨ 20–39%   ■ 40–59%   ▨ > 60%

Table 3.1: The effectiveness of a manager (Garratt-Gnann et al. 1997)

The role of the manager

Critical incident 17

What do you think is happening here?

(This example is taken from Triandis (1975: 42–3), who found it in the files of a Greek psychiatrist.)

A US manager (A) has a Greek subordinate (G). A report has to be written.

A How long will it take you to finish this report?

G I do not know. How long should it take?

A You are in the best position to analyse time requirements.

G Ten days.

A Take 15. So is it agreed you will do it in 15 days?

In fact, the report needed 30 days of regular work. So the Greek member of staff worked day and night, but at the end of the 15th day, he still needed one more day's work.

A Where is my report?

G It will be ready tomorrow.

A But we agreed it would be ready today.

At this point, the Greek hands in his resignation.

Comments

The general problem is that there are two different concepts of the roles of the manager and the subordinate. A feels that the subordinate should be involved in decision-making, whereas G expects to be told what to do. A technique used by psychologists, called ATTRIBUTION analysis, can be used to explain the causes of this problem in more detail. Essentially, communication breaks down because both of the co-workers attribute different meanings to what their partner says, but assume that the other worker understands the same as they do.

Behaviour	Attribution
A How long will it take you to finish this report?	A I asked him to participate. G His behaviour makes no sense. He is the boss. Why doesn't he tell me?
G I do not know. How long should it take?	A He refuses to take responsibility.
A You are in the best position to analyse time requirements.	A I press him to take responsibility for his own actions.
G Ten days	G What nonsense! I'd better give him an answer. He lacks the ability to estimate time; this estimate is totally inadequate.
A Take 15. So is it agreed you will do it in 15 days?	A I offer him a contract. G These are my orders. 15 days.
A Where is my report?	A I am making sure he fulfills his contract.
G It will be ready tomorrow.	G He is asking for the report. (Both attribute that it is not ready.)
A But we had agreed that it would be ready today.	A I must teach him to fulfill a contract. G The stupid, incompetent boss! Not only did he give me the wrong orders, but he does not appreciate that I did a 30-day job in 16 days.
The Greek hands in his resignation.	The American is surprised. G I can't work for such a man.

Table 3.2: Behaviour and attribution (Triandis 1975)

A manager's role varies across cultures

Laurent (1983) asked people if they agreed or disagreed with the following statement:
'It is important for a manager to have at hand precise answers to most of the questions that his subordinates may raise about their work.' The results of his survey are shown in Figure 3.1.

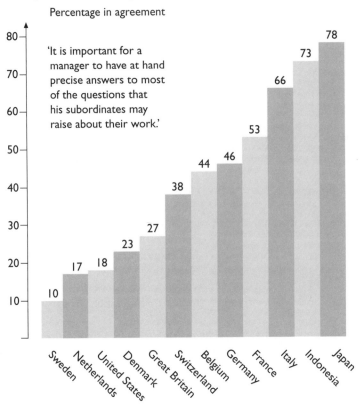

Figure 3.1: Managers' roles across cultures (Laurent 1983)

Exercise 17

Why might Laurent's findings be of interest to managers and staff? Where might the differences his research points to come from?

Suggested answer

There could well be frustrations in teams made up of those people who are low down on the scale, and those who are high on the scale. Tensions will occur, for instance, if a US manager only gives general answers to his Indonesian subordinates, who might be expecting him to provide them with precise answers. Some of the differences are due to the fact that managers are trained differently in different cultures: for instance, many British managers had a general education, and might have studied a subject unconnected with business, whereas in other cultures managers may have studied Business Administration, or a technical subject that is closely linked to their later work.

Exercise 18

How do you think managers from different countries would react to the following situations?

1 The morale of the people in the department is low. There are personal conflicts, and people feel the workload is too high.
2 A member of the department complains that a colleague is not doing his job properly, and that this is having a negative effect on the performance of the team.
3 A product made by the department has won a prize as the best in its field.

Suggested answers

There are many different ways of reacting. Research conducted in an international computer company showed the different ways in which managers from Britain, USA, Germany, and France saw these situations.

1 Representatives from all four cultures tended to stress the need to get the team to work together and communicate better, as well as to define priorities. While the Germans suggested reorganizing the department, the British felt that the manager should sympathize with the staff, and be a friend to them, and the French stressed the need for decisions to be made. For their part, the US managers suggested bringing in help from the outside.

2 Representatives from each of the four cultures tended to say that action had to be taken, and that it was important to hear both sides of the story. The British said that it was important to be diplomatic and tactful, and suggested the need to find out whether the colleague has any personal problems which might be affecting their performance at work. The French and Germans agreed that it was important to check on the workload, and to remove any obstacles. The Americans stressed the need to 'coach and clarify', and to take the problem seriously.

3 Representatives from all four cultures agreed that there should be some form of celebration. The Germans and French favoured congratulating the whole team, while many of the British and Americans thought that they should be congratulated individually. The Americans thought that the source of their success should be looked at, so that they could be used to influence the development of other parts of the organization.

(Adapted from Garratt-Gnann *et al.* 1997: 113–8)

Organizational structure

Hofstede has related his dimensions of power distance and uncertainty avoidance to organizational structures, which in turn influence the role of managers. Figure 3.2 shows five examples of cultures and typical organizational structures:

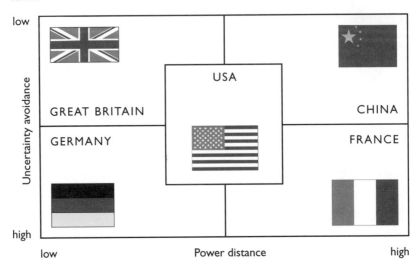

Figure 3.2: Power distance and uncertainty avoidance

Great Britain, with small power distance, and weak uncertainty avoidance, favours the 'village market' type of structure. Problems are solved by managers and staff working together as they arise.

Germany, with small power distance and strong uncertainty avoidance, favours the 'well-oiled machine', with a more bureaucratic structure than the British, and a professionally trained staff. This is illustrated by the existence of the highly developed system of vocational training.

France, with large power distance, and strong uncertainty avoidance, favours a 'pyramid of people', with a hierarchical bureaucracy and standardized work processes.

China, with large power distance and weak uncertainty avoidance, favours the 'family' approach, with direct supervision by the owner of the company and relatives.

The USA is in the middle of the matrix, and favours organization in divisions, with a standardization of output.

Trompenaars presents the hierarchies in different cultures in another way in Figure 3.3.

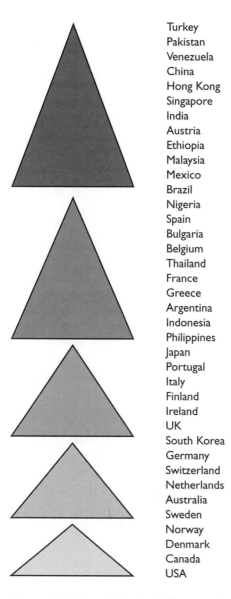

Turkey
Pakistan
Venezuela
China
Hong Kong
Singapore
India
Austria
Ethiopia
Malaysia
Mexico
Brazil
Nigeria
Spain
Bulgaria
Belgium
Thailand
France
Greece
Argentina
Indonesia
Philippines
Japan
Portugal
Italy
Finland
Ireland
UK
South Korea
Germany
Switzerland
Netherlands
Australia
Sweden
Norway
Denmark
Canada
USA

Figure 3.3: Hierarchies in different cultures (Trompenaars and Hampden-Turner 1997)

Managers working in organizations abroad, or with partners from organizations with a different culture, must be aware of these differences if they are to function effectively.

Cultural checklist: managing people
- How do staff see the role of the manager?
- How much are managers expected to know about the details of the job?
- What is the educational background of managers in the cultures you are dealing with?
- How can the manager motivate staff?
- How can conflicts be dealt with?
- How strong are hierarchies?

Negotiating

A good negotiator

Exercise 19
What do you think makes a good negotiator?

Suggested answer
Just as different cultures differ about how they see the role of the manager, they also have different approaches to negotiation. This section explores some of the cultural factors that influence negotiations, and suggests some ways of dealing with them.

What is negotiation?
Negotiation can be defined as the process of bargaining between two or more parties to reach a solution that is acceptable to all parties.

Casse and Deol (1985) identify three types of negotiation:

1 negotiation based on compromise
2 negotiation based on synthesis (all ideas are taken into account)
3 negotiation based on synergy (the result is greater than the sum of the parts).

Exercise 20

What do you think are the advantages and disadvantages of the three types of negotiation?

Suggested answer
Type 1: compromise
Advantages: the negotiators can overcome problems and move forward faster.

Disadvantages: those who have to give up something may get frustrated. This might lead to a lack of commitment to the final decision.

Type 2: synthesis
Advantages: the negotiators try to integrate all the ideas in the final agreement. This leads to motivation and commitment.

Disadvantages: sometimes irrelevant elements are included in the decision, which can weaken the outcome of the negotiation, and make it more questionable.

Type 3: synergy
Advantages: the outcome of the negotiation is the creative product of the interaction. It is a 'win–win' situation.

Disadvantages: this requires a lot of time, as well as a high level of flexibility, and open minds.

(Adapted from Casse and Deol 1985: 41)

Culture and negotiation

There are various stages in a negotiation, each of which can be affected by cultural factors. Stages commonly identified include:

- relationship building
- agreeing procedure
- exchanging information
- questioning
- options
- bidding
- bargaining
- settling and concluding.

(O'Connor *et al.* 1992)

Of course, the stages may not come in the order given. The list is itself culturally bound, since it suggests a linear approach to negotiation. In some cultures several stages would occur at the same time, or not at all.

Some cultures will spend a long time on building relations, and getting to know the negotiating partner, before getting down to business, while others get down to business straight away. In monochronic cultures, time will be spent on setting time limits, and possibly on allotting time for items on the agenda. More information will be exchanged in low-context cultures than in high-context ones, whereas in some other cultures direct questions can be perceived as rude, and therefore best avoided. In high-power distance cultures, only people high up in the hierarchy will be allowed to make decisions. In collectivist cultures, by contrast, there will be a need for consensus from the whole team. The practice of bidding—to what extent it is acceptable to bargain, and what form the bargaining should take—varies widely across cultures. Even the final agreement can vary from being a contract which is legally binding in every detail, to a general statement of co-operation, with the precise details changing according to changing circumstances.

Casse and Deol summarize cultural assumptions related to negotiation in Table 3.3.

		CULTURES		
	ASSUMPTIONS	JAPANESE	NORTH AMERICA	LATIN AMERICA
1	Emotions	Emotions are valued, but must be hidden.	Emotions are not highly valued. Transactions with others are mostly un-emotional.	Emotional sensitivity is valued. Interactions can be highly emotional and even passionate.
2	Power	Subtle power plays. Conciliation is sought.	Power games are played all the time. Litigation, not so much conciliation. To be strong is highly valued.	Great power plays. To be stronger than the others is particularly valued.
3	Decision making	Group decision making.	Teamwork provides inputs to decision makers.	Decisions are made by individuals in charge.
4	Social interaction	Face-saving is crucial. Decisions are often made on the basis of saving someone from embarrassment.	Decisions are made on a cost/benefit basis. Face-saving does not openly matter.	Face-saving for oneself is critical to preserve honor and dignity.
5	Persuasion	Not very argumentative. Quiet when right. Respecful and patient. Modesty and self-restraint are highly valued.	Argumentative when right or wrong. Impersonal when arguing. Practical when presenting arguments.	Passionate and emotional when arguing. Enjoy a warm interaction as well as a lively debate.

Table 3.3: Cultural assumptions related to negotiation (Casse and Deol 1985)

Exercise 21

What cultural dimensions (see Chapter 2) are behind these different statements?

1 I've booked a table at a wonderful restaurant. Let's go there first and continue the negotiations after lunch.
2 We will finish at 5.30. That gives us 15 minutes for item 1, 20 minutes for item 2 . . .
3 We need to discuss the matter with each other before we can come to an agreement.
4 I'd like to start by going around the table and asking each person to say what they think about the problem.
5 The boss isn't here—I suggest we cancel the meeting.
6 I disagree with your idea.
7 Let's talk about the details later—first we should agree on some general principles.

Suggested answers
1 Person and task. This person puts value on building up relationships first, before getting down to business.
2 Time. This illustrates a linear approach to time: the negotiation will be tightly structured and contributions not strictly relevant will be stopped.
3 Individual and group. This is a collectivist approach—the group has to be consulted before a decision can be made. A delegation of several people, rather than an individual, will take part in the negotiation.
4 Power. Here power distance is low—the views of all the people present are equally valid, regardless of their position in the hierarchy.
5 Power. Here power distance is high—no decision is possible without the presence of the person at the top of the hierarchy.
6 Communication style: directness. This person makes a direct statement rather than expressing disagreement through body language, or even silence.
7 Context. This is a high-context approach. The general ideas are of more importance than the details, which can be dealt with later.

Meetings

Lewis (1996) illustrates some different communication styles found in national cultures in meetings.

Exercise 22

Look at Figure 3.4 and try to work out which national cultures each of the three diagrams describes. Give reasons for your answer.

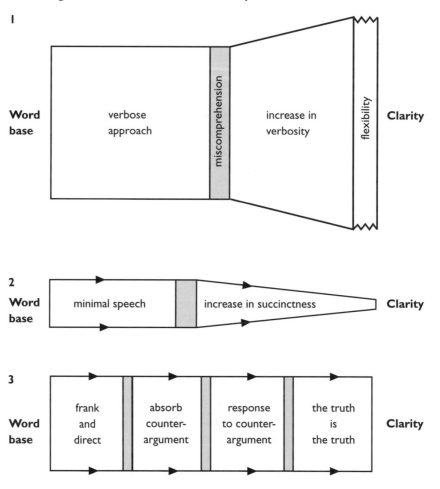

Figure 3.4: Communication styles (Lewis 1996)

Suggested answers

1 This is supposed to illustrate an Italian communication style. The more there is a problem in the negotiation, the more words are used.
2 This is supposed to illustrate a Finnish communication style, where problems are dealt with by using fewer words.
3 This is supposed to illustrate a German communication style.

Exercise 23

How useful are the diagrams in Figure 3.4 for helping us to understand cultural differences in communication style?

Suggested answer

This visual representation of communication can be very useful. However, questions should be asked as to where the ideas behind the diagrams come from—are they based on research into discourse, or on anecdotes? Is there a danger of merely reproducing stereotypes, made convincing by the fact that they are presented in the form of attractive diagrams? At the very least, they can be a useful basis for discussion.

Contracts

Critical incident 18

What do you think is happening here?

> After extremely long negotiations, the US delegation was pleased to see that the contract for a new joint venture project with their Chinese partners was ready to be signed. They were particularly impressed that the Chinese had invited local dignitaries to the signing ceremony. Everything went smoothly until work on the new factory was supposed to begin. It was found that the Chinese were not following the conditions laid down in the contract, and had even suggested further negotiations.

Comments

The use of a contract is seen very differently in China and the USA. In the USA it comes at the end of negotiations, and lays down the rights and duties of all the parties involved, while in China, where relationships are valued highly, it is seen more as a general declaration of mutual trust, and is celebrated (hence the invitation of the local dignitaries) as such. In China it is seen as quite acceptable to change things to fit changing circumstances, and, where necessary, to renegotiate parts of the contract. This approach to the contract explains why Chinese negotiations last a long time—the negotiation and entertainment of the business partners is seen as a process of getting to know each other. The business details are of secondary importance.

Cultural checklist: negotiating

- Where does the negotiation take place? In the office, a restaurant, or on the golf course?
- How many people are involved in the negotiation?
- Where do people sit? How far apart do they sit?
- What is the appropriate dress? Casual or formal wear?
- What is the role of the chairperson?
- How far can emotions be shown?
- Is it more appropriate to argue or to remain silent?
- Is there an agenda? How far is it kept to?
- How important is time-keeping?

- Are decisions made by individuals or by the group?
- Is the maintaining of relationships more important than making a decision?
- How can you prevent people from 'losing face'?
- How do the different participants see the agreement? What is included in a contract? What does a contract mean to the various parties?

Socializing

Often the hardest part of doing business is not the deal itself, but all that surrounds it. The approach varies greatly from culture to culture. In some contexts it is quite acceptable to get down to business right away, while in others it is important to build relationships first. Attitudes to socializing, and the division between public and private spheres, also differ. This unit helps you to become more aware of some of these factors.

Critical incident 19

What do you think is happening here?

> Hans Braun is on a business trip to the USA, and things seem to be going well. In fact, it looks like he will have some time to relax at the weekend before returning to Germany. He asks his American colleague, Joe Webb, for some tips on what to do. Joe immediately offers him the use of the family cabin in the mountains, as well as his car. Hans Braun is amazed at the generosity of his colleague, who he only met a few days before, but says he can't possibly accept. He hires a car and books into a hotel. Joe can't understand this behaviour. Hans Braun is surprised.

Comments
This situation can be explained by using the model of the peach and the coconut (see Figure 3.5).

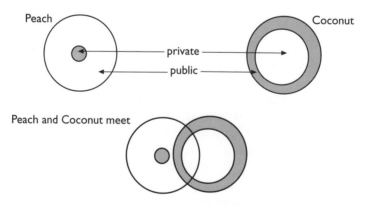

Figure 3.5: The peach and the coconut model (adapted from Zaninelli 1994)

In the United States (shown by the peach) the public sphere is relatively large, with a small private sphere. First names are used immediately, even in business; Joe Webb offers his cabin and car to someone he doesn't even know very well. In Germany (shown by the coconut) the private sphere is much larger, and hard to get into. Surnames and titles are used even by colleagues who have worked together for years; the private sphere is reserved for special friends. The problem comes when they meet: Hans Braun interprets the offer of the car and cabin as a sign of special friendship which can't exist after only a few days; he is also worried that he doesn't feel in a position to pay back the generosity. For Joe Webb it is nothing special, and doesn't mean that they are special friends; he doesn't expect his kindness to be paid back. The definition of friendship is fundamentally different.

Exercise 24

The coconut and the peach can perceive each other positively or negatively. Below is a discussion of how they could see each other negatively. Think how they could perceive the same behaviour in a positive way.

Negative

The coconut sees the peach as:

- superficial
- too playful
- not to be taken seriously, childish
- insincere

The peach sees the coconut as:

- unapproachable
- stiff
- lacking humour
- hard
- impolite
- gruff

Suggested answer
Positive
The coconut sees the peach as:

- open
- friendly
- flexible
- enthusiastic
- humorous

The peach sees the coconut as:

- reliable
- clear
- trustworthy
- proper
- honest

(Adapted from Zaninelli 1994: 97–100)

Critical incident 20

What do you think is happening here?

Following the takeover of a British car manufacturer by a leading German company, Günther Hoffmann has been sent to Britain to find out why productivity in the plant in the Midlands is so low. The managers seem to work long hours—many are still in the office at 7.00 pm, but they waste their day in endless meetings. They don't seem to take work that seriously, and every phone call ends up in small talk about what they did at the weekend. It is the final straw when one of the British managers, having failed to give Dr. Hoffmann the information he wanted, suggests talking about the problem in the pub after work. No wonder they've got problems with productivity!

Comments

This case brings out several differences between doing business in Britain and Germany. Research (Stewart *et al.* 1994) shows that middle managers in Germany tend to work more of the day on their own than their British counterparts. For the British, it isn't a meeting that is an annoying extra, but the work itself. Great stress is put on brainstorming ideas together, and building up the team. The chat about the weekend is also part of this process, as is the invitation to the pub. This social exchange is seen as a part of 'oiling the machine', so that people can work together effectively. The division between work and pleasure is not as strict as it can be in Germany—it is quite normal to socialize with your colleagues. There is no English equivalent for the German saying: *Dienst ist Dienst und Schnaps ist Schnaps*, ('Work is work, and schnaps is schnaps'). British people working in Germany may miss this social contact with colleagues, and interpret it as unfriendliness.

Critical incident 21

What do you think is happening here?

The demands of socializing can put the business person under great pressure. A senior manager of a German car manufacturer gave his first impressions after his posting to Japan:

'When I arrived in Tokyo everything was well prepared. But two comments of my predecessor puzzled me. First, westerners have almost no chance of understanding Japan, and they will always be treated as unwelcome foreigners. Second, in any case I would have to change my lifestyle completely. If I wanted to get familiar with our Japanese car dealers, I would be obliged to drink at least 70 to 80 glasses of *sake* with each of them. Additionally, I would have to be out each night. Let me put it this way: intercultural competence through drinking.'

How would you cope with this situation?

Critical incident 22

What do you think is happening here?

Craig Storti tells the story of a US couple invited to a Moroccan family home for dinner:

Having pressed their host to fix a time, they arrive half an hour late, and are shown into the guest room. After a decent interval, they ask after the host's wife, who has yet to appear, and are told that she's busy in the kitchen. At one point their host's little son wanders in, and the couple remark on his good looks. Just before the meal is served, the guests ask to be shown to the toilet so they may wash their hands. The main course is served in and eaten from a large platter, and the couple choose morsels of food from wherever they can reach, trying to keep up polite conversation throughout the meal. Soon after the tea and cookies, they take their leave.

(Storti 1990: 24–5)

Comments

Storti explains what they did wrong:

Almost everything. They confused their host by asking him to fix the hour, for in the Moslem world an invitation to a meal is really an invitation to come and spend time with your friends, during the course of which time, God willing, a meal may very well appear. To ask what time you should come is tantamount to asking your host how long he wants you around, and implies, as well, that you are more interested in the meal than in having his company.

One should be careful about asking after a Moslem man's wife; often she would not eat with foreign guests, even if female spouses were present, and might not even be introduced. In any case, her place would usually be in the kitchen, guaranteeing that the meal is as good as she can produce, thereby showing respect for her guests, and bringing honour on her and her husband's house. Nor should one praise the intelligence and good looks of small children, in case this might alert evil spirits to the presence of a prized object in the home, so that they might come and cause harm. It was not appropriate to ask for the toilet either, for a decorative basin would have been offered for the washing of hands (and the nicer it is, the more honour it conveys upon the family). Nor should one talk during the meal; it interferes with the enjoyment of the food to have to keep up a conversation, and may even be interpreted as a slight against the cooking. Guests should only take the food from the part of the platter directly in front of them, and not from anywhere else within their reach. Not only is it rude to reach, but doing so deprives the host of one of his chief duties and pleasures: finding the best pieces of chicken and lamb, and ostentatiously placing them before the guest.

(Storti 1990: 25)

Cultural checklist: socializing

- How far are business and pleasure mixed?
- Where does socializing take place? In the office? On the golf course? In the sauna? In a restaurant? In a pub or bar? At someone's home? Other places?
- Who pays?
- What topics are talked about? Is it rude to mention business? What topics are taboo?
- Who takes part in the social activity? People of the same level in the hierarchy? People of different levels? Are partners (husbands/wives) included?

Giving presentations

A good presentation

Exercise 25

Imagine you are going to give a business presentation. What do you think about the following techniques?

1 starting with a joke
2 reading a written text
3 involving the audience
4 keeping to the time limit
5 making the structure very clear
6 providing the audience with handouts
7 dressing formally
8 looking serious
9 only taking questions at the end of the presentation
10 using visual aids (for example, a beamer or overhead projector)
11 summarizing what you have said at the end of the presentation
12 telling anecdotes

This exercise will help you to be more aware of your own presentation style. The next one looks at how different cultures see presentations.

Critical incident 23

What do you think is happening here?

An international group of business people is listening to a sales presentation. The speaker takes off his jacket, starts with a quick joke, and then follows the KISS principle ('Keep It Short and Simple'), illustrating his words with lively computer graphics. He invites the audience to interrupt with their questions, and when they don't he smiles broadly at them and starts to ask them questions. Like all good presenters—or so he thinks—he tells the audience what he is going to say, then says it, and then tells them what he has said. He keeps exactly to the 10 minutes allotted. The reaction of the audience is mixed: some are impressed, others feel unhappy with it.

Comments

The speaker has failed to adapt his presentation to the international nature of his audience. While his approach would be acceptable in many settings in the USA or the UK, people from other cultures may find it too informal (taking off his jacket, making jokes, smiling). For some, the speaker's concern for the audience (seen in the use of graphics to convey information, and his attempt to get questions from them) was at the cost of the content, which they would have found too superficial. The explicit structure, too, would irritate some members of the audience, while others might feel that the rigid time-keeping was unnecessary.

Types of presentation

There are, of course, many different types of presentation. The word is used rather loosely in English.

The type of presentation will depend on a number of factors, including not only the national culture of the speaker and the audience, but also the professional and corporate culture. A sales presentation, for instance, may well be very different from a more technical one given by an engineer. In the same way, some presentations focus on the information that is being presented, while others focus on persuading the audience.

Culture and presentations

A Belgian Professor in Business Communication writes about presentation style:

> French-speaking Belgians tend to see a presentation rather as the French do, in a polychronic and implicit way, with a set, but not explicit, structure. Language fluency is very important, and according to the rules of classical rhetoric, the right word should be used. The aesthetic aspect of the presentation is more important than the structure of the content. A presentation should be a logical progression, based on large philosophical or ideological ideas. The importance of what is being said—the content—lies in the way it is presented: one's objective is not to be clear and simple, but to be creative and provoking, to make the audience think and reason. Body language is considered to be part of the presentation, and presenters are usually advised to limit the amount of gesturing, but not the scope: move your arms from the shoulders onwards, and not just from the elbows.
>
> (Claes, M.-T., in Bennett *et al.* 1998: 126–7)

Exercise 26

Think about how the Belgian described here might react to the presentation described in Critical incident 23.

Suggested answer

They might find the presentation superficial and impersonal. They would want more depth of communication.

There are significant differences between monochronic and polychronic presentations, as well as those in low- and high-context cultures. Figure 3.6 shows some of these differences.

Structures of a presentation

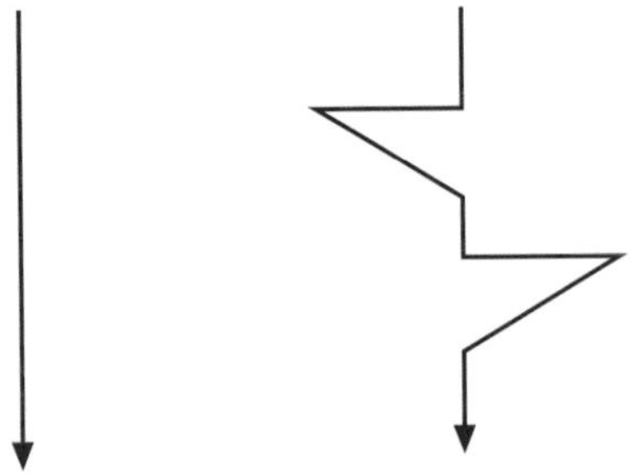

Anglo-Saxon   Latin

	Anglo-Saxon	Latin
Orientation	Presenting: static Audience-orientated: • structure, facts • not involved personally • matter-of-fact	Convincing: mobile Speaker-orientated: • intutition • involved, passionate • loose structure
Mode of reasoning	Direct: • confrontation-centred • rational • practical empiricism	Indirect: • agreement-centred • intuitive • harmony

Figure 3.6: Structures of a presentation (Claes 2000)

Coping with an international audience

Exercise 27

How would you go about giving a business presentation to an international audience?

Suggested answer

It is probably easier to describe the differences in presentation style than to cope with them effectively. As with other elements of intercultural communication, the first step is to be aware of your own style, and the effect it might have on other people. It is difficult, and probably not desirable, to try to imitate another style (remember the Japanese saying 'The crow that imitates the cormorant drowns in the water'). However, you can at least try to limit or build on elements of your style, according to how you think the audience might react. A German presenter, for instance, might leave out some historical background and detail when presenting to a US audience. In any given situation, it can also help to show the audience that, while you are aware of your own cultural background, you understand that they may have a different personal style.

It is important to adapt your language to your audience, so if you are speaking in English, make sure that your audience will understand. Here are some tips on how to do this:

- Avoid idioms.
- Speak more slowly and clearly than you might do with native speakers.
- Stress important words.
- Make your structure clear to the audience.
- Check whether the audience is following your arguments.
- Support your argument with visuals.

Cultural checklist: giving presentations

- Language: formal or informal. Level of audience.
- Structure: linear or digressive. Explicit or implicit.
- Content: detailed or general.
- Delivery: text read or improvised.
- Timing: fixed or flexible.
- Audience: oriented to audience or speaker.
- Dress: formal or informal.
- Behaviour: serious or relaxed.

Advertising

Content

Exercise 28

What problems might the following TV advert cause in some markets?

A woman is shown coming out of the shower and getting dressed. In the following scene, a man is seen taking flowers from a restaurant table. In the final scene, the man gives the flowers to the woman, they look into each other's eyes, and leave together.

Suggested answer
The advertisers of the deodorant 'Impulse' made different advertisements for different markets. While in some cultures the woman could be shown semi-naked, in others she was shown fully clothed. In some versions of the advertisement the man bought the flowers from the market, since otherwise, taking the flowers from the restaurant, however impulsively, would be seen as stealing. In some of the different versions, the couple didn't look at each other directly, and the woman left by herself.

Advertisers need to consider such cultural differences when planning their campaigns. Although they might not run a global campaign with exactly the same advertisement all over the world, they can take advantage of Hofstede's dimensions, for instance, as a tool to segment the market.

Clusters of similar markets can be identified. An example shows how this could look in Europe:

Cluster 1
Austria, Germany, Switzerland, Italy, the UK, and the Irish Republic

These countries have small power distance, medium uncertainty avoidance, medium–high individualism, and high masculinity.

Advertising in these areas should stress high performance and successful achiever themes.

Cluster 2
Belgium, France, Greece, Portugal, Spain, Turkey

These countries have medium power distance, strong uncertainty avoidance, varied individualism, and low–medium masculinity.

Advertising here should appeal to the consumer's status, emphasize the functionality of the product, and stress risk-reduction features, such as guarantees, or the possibility of returning the goods if not satisfied.

Cluster 3
Denmark, Sweden, Finland, Netherlands, Norway

These countries have small power distance, low uncertainty avoidance, high individualism, and low–medium masculinity.

Here advertisers can expect strong consumer enthusiasm for novelty and variety, and high concern for socially conscious companies and environmentally friendly products.

(Adapted from Kale 1995: 42)

Language

Exercise 29

What problems might the following cause in some markets?

1 The General Motors car called 'Nova'.
2 The slogan for a vacuum cleaner 'Nothing sucks like an Electrolux'.
3 IBM series 44 computers.

Suggested answers

1 This name would not be suitable for Spanish-speaking markets, because its meaning would be 'it doesn't go'. Similarly, the English word 'mist' for a perfume would not be suitable for the German market, because in German the word means 'manure'. The Mitsubishi 'Pajero' is a rude word in Spanish, and therefore not suitable for that market, while in Britain, the Lancia 'Dedra' was associated with death. The Fiat 'Uno' was not suitable for Finland because in Finnish it means 'fool'. Bahlsen found that while their product name for a biscuit called 'Kipferl' didn't work in France, because people couldn't pronounce the word, the same product became successful under the name 'Croissant de Lune'. 'Nike' is a swear word in Arabic.

2 This slogan is open to two meanings—the first suggests that the vacuum cleaner sucks up the dirt, but in American English it would be confused with an impolite expression which is used to suggest that something is extremely bad.

3 In Japan the series had to be given a different number, because the number 4 is associated with death. Positive connotations of numbers can also be used for effect in advertising. For instance, Mercedes chose to call one of its cars the C88, and thus exploited the fact that in China the number 8 is considered to be lucky, and it is also considered lucky to have a double number.

As some of the above examples suggest, when planning an advertisement to be used internationally, it is important to think about the possible implications right from the beginning. It is not enough to produce something in one language, and then find someone to translate it. Even the physical layout of text on the page needs to be considered carefully, since the length of text will vary from language to language. The copywriter needs to allow for the fact that the translated version of an English-language text will be 20–25% longer in French and Italian, and 25–30% longer in German.

Visuals

Exercise 30

What problems might the following cause in some markets? Why?

The advertisement for pain killers that shows three pictures from left to right: first, someone with a headache, who is next seen taking the pain killer and, finally, smiling.

Suggested answer

This advertisement would be unsuitable for cultures in which people read from right to left, since the message conveyed would be the opposite of what was intended. A similar advertisement produced by Lucky Goldstar showed a rice bowl on the left-hand side of the page, and a satellite on the right.

Exercise 31

What do the following symbols found on web sites mean to you?

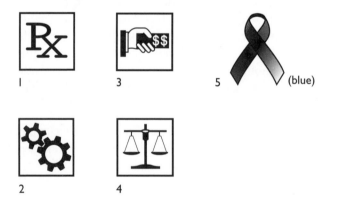

Figure 3.7: The use of imagery and symbols (Pauwels 2000)

Comments

Research was done into what these symbols mean to people from different cultures. The results showed that some of the symbols were far from universally understood.

1 was supposed to indicate 'pharmaceutical', but many people in the survey thought it stood for 'peace', 'Christianity', or something else.
2 was intended to mean 'manufacturing', and was correctly interpreted as such by the majority in the survey.
3 was supposed to mean 'financial', but was also interpreted as indicating 'illegal earnings', or 'black market'.
4 was supposed to mean 'justice', and was seen as such by most participants in the survey.
5 was supposed to mean 'free speech', but many people thought it meant something else, such as 'an award', 'homosexual', or 'Aids'.

(Pauwels 2000: 272–4)

Focus groups from the USA and some European countries were asked by web designers to react to two common icons: the 'buy' button and the shopping basket.

BUY

Europeans were negative about the 'buy' button, and more likely to buy using the shopping basket icon. This suggests that you can reverse your decision and take the item out of the basket, as opposed to the finality of the decision suggested by the 'buy' symbol. This could be explained by Hofstede's concept of 'uncertainty avoidance' (see p. 48).

How far meaning is expressed through visuals, and how far through words, also varies across cultures. Research comparing web sites for the same company in different countries has shown that they differ widely in the way information is presented. In the USA, more use was made of icons and graphics than in other cultures, where there was more use of text. In China, companies are advised to include more people in their publicity material, and if possible to show Chinese dignitaries visiting the company—a tactic which reflects the importance of personal contacts in China.

Colours

Advertisers also have to take into account what associations different cultures have with different colours, and to take care which colours are used in advertising or packaging materials.

Exercise 32

What do you associate with the following colours?

1 white
2 black
3 red

4 green
5 purple

Suggested answers

1 White can be used in the West to indicate birth, or other happy events, while in China it is linked with death.
2 Black is associated in the West with death, but has no such meaning in China.
3 Red is the colour of blood, but can be interpreted to mean 'life' or 'death'.
4 In the USA, green is used to indicate freshness and health, but in some cultures it is associated with dangerous jungles—it is even forbidden in some parts of Indonesia.
5 In the USA, purple indicates that something is inexpensive, whereas in some parts of Asia it means the opposite.

Cultural checklist: advertising

- Check that the brand or product name is acceptable in target markets.
- Be careful with slogans that might not work in other languages, or in other areas of the English-speaking world.
- Respect taboos and customs.
- Avoid references which will not be understood by people from other cultures.
- Check that symbols or icons are understood in the target markets in the way that you intend them.
- Consider the balance between text and visuals. This may need to change as you move into other cultures.
- Allow for the fact that the length of text will vary from language to language.

How effective would this advertisement be in your culture?

Applying for a job

Exercise 33

Which of the following should you do when applying for a job?

1 Include references and certificates.
2 Sign and date your curriculum vitae.
3 Include details of your family.
4 Attach a photograph of yourself to the application.
5 Include details of hobbies and leisure interests.

Comments

The accepted way of applying for jobs varies widely across national cultures, and within different areas of business. The approach you make to an advertising agency, for instance, might not be at all suitable if you were approaching a bank.

1 In the UK and the USA it is not usual to send references and certificates with a job application. References which the applicant has seen (so-called 'testimonials') are not considered to be of much value. Many prospective employers prefer to have the name, address, and telephone number of the candidate's previous employers, so that they can be contacted on a confidential basis.

2 In the UK and USA it is not usual to sign or date your résumé or curriculum vitae.

3 Details of your family (for example, your parents' professions) are not normally seen as having any relevance in the UK and USA. The employer is more concerned with what *you* have done and can do, rather than your family background.

4 Photographs should not be included in the UK and USA unless specifically asked for. Often this is because of equal opportunity programmes in companies that want to make sure they are not discriminating on the basis of the colour of the applicant's skin. In some companies, applicants are asked not to include any indication of their gender, to ensure that there is no sexual discrimination.

5 In Britain and the USA, hobbies and leisure interests are seen as relevant, since they tell the employer about the applicant's personality. Involvement in a football team, for instance, can indicate that the candidate is able to work in a team. Don't include too many hobbies, however, otherwise the employer might wonder if you are more interested in sport than in work.

Exercise 34

Look at the curriculum vitae below (written by a German student in the style of a British CV) and say how it is different from a similar document in your culture.

CHRISTINA KLEIN

CONTACT DETAILS

Auf der Schanz 49
85049 Ingolstadt
Germany
Tel/Fax.: 0841 937 5987
christina.klein@t-online.de

PERSONAL DATA

Date of Birth: 12.03.77
Nationality: German

EDUCATION

07.2000

Diploma in Business Administration, Grade 1.3 (very good)

10.1995 – 07.2000

Ingolstadt School of Business, Germany
Student of Business Administration
Diploma thesis: Cultural factors in mergers and acquisitions
Options: International Management, Finance

01.1998 – 06.1998	European Business School, London
10.1997 – 12.1997	EDHEC, Lille, France
06.1995	Abitur (university entrance requirement), Grade 1.7 (good)
09.1988 – 06.1995	Goethe Gymnasium, Munich

WORK EXPERIENCE

08. – 09.1999	Deutsche Bank, Frankfurt
	Project assistant in securities trading department
03. – 04.1999	Creditanstalt, New York
	Financial analysis of investment banks
07. – 09.1998	Deutsche Morgan Grenfell, London
	Assistant in corporate finance department

LANGUAGES	German (native speaker); English (fluent); French (fluent); Spanish (good working knowledge); Japanese (basic knowledge).
SKILLS	Experienced designer of internet websites Full driving licence
ACHIEVEMENTS	Elected as student representative on the faculty board. Organised fundraising for victims of Kosovo war; raised DM 25,000. Run summer sport camps for children
LEISURE	Tennis, basketball, swimming; travel

Further reading

Negotiating

A book for learning the English of negotiating, which also contains material on dealing with cultural differences, is:

O'Connor, P., A. Pilbeam, and **F. Scott-Barrett.** *Negotiating.* Harlow: Longman.

Presentations

An interesting book on this subject, which was developed by communication specialists from some top European business schools, and comes with a video of student presentations is:

Bennett *et al.* 1998. *Doing Effective Presentations in an Intercultural Setting.* Vienna: Ueberreuter.

Marketing

A key book on the importance of culture in international marketing, which has excellent sections on a range of communication issues, including advertising, is:

Usunier, J.-C. 1993. *International Marketing: A Cultural Approach.* Hemel Hempstead: Prentice Hall.

Applying for a job

A highly successful book which is updated every year, and shows a US approach to finding a job, is:

Bolles, R. 2001. *What Color is your Parachute?* Berkeley: Ten Speed Press.

4 CULTURES

Your culture

Before looking at other cultures, it is important to reflect on your own culture.

In his poem 'To a Louse', the Scottish poet Robert Burns (1759–96) wrote:

> O wad some Pow'r the giftie gie us
> To see ourselves as others see us!
> It wad frae mony a blunder free us,
> And foolish notion.

(Oh would some power give us the gift, to see ourselves as others see us! It would free us from many a blunder and foolish notion.)

The idea of providing information about cultures for travellers is not new. In the 18th century, so-called *Völkertafel* (literally 'tables of peoples'), with descriptions of people in different countries, were to be found in inns in Germany and Austria (see page 84).

The modern equivalent is the guide to local customs and good manners for business people working abroad. Since many such professionals have little time to prepare for their foreign assignments, these guides tend to be short and oversimplified lists of dos and don'ts, and so run the risk of reinforcing stereotypes.

Exercise 35

Before reading about cultures that are different to your own, think about what you would tell people from other cultures about your own culture. What would you tell them about the following?

A Cultural dimensions (see Chapter 2)

1 non-verbal communication
2 communication style
3 time and space
4 power
5 the individual and the group
6 uncertainty
7 nature

	Spanier.	Frantzoß.	Wälisch.	Teutscher.	Engerländer.	Schwöd.	Polack.	Unger.	Muskowith.	Türk
Kurze Beschreibung der In Europa Befintlichen Völckern Und Ihren Eigenschafften										
Namen.	Spanier.	Frantzoß.	Wälisch.	Teutscher.	Engerländer.	Schwöd.	Polack.	Unger.	Muskowith.	Türk od...
Sitten, Und Natur Eigenschafft	Hochmüttig,	Leichtsinig,	Hinderhaltig,	Offenhertzig,	Wohlgestalt,	Starck und Groß,	Bäurisch,	Untreu,	Boßhafft,	Übrilu...
Verständ.	Klug und Weiß,	Fürsichtig,	Scharffsinig,	Witzig,	Anmuthig,	Hartknäfig,	Gering Achtent,	Nochweniger,	Gar Nichts,	Oben...
Anzeügung dern Eigenschafften	Männlich,	Kindisch,	Wiejederwill,	Über Allmit,	Weiblich,	Unerfendlich,	Mittlmässig,	Bluthbegirig,	Unentlichrob,	Zärt...
Wissenschafft.	schrifftgelehrt,	In Kriegssachen	Geistlichen Rechte	Weltlichen Rechte	Welt Weis,	Freuen Künsten	lichen Sprachen	Lateinischer Sprach	Griechischer Sprach	Vollit...
Der Kleidung (Tracht)	Ehrbaar,	Unbeständig,	Ehrsam,	Machtalles Nach	auf Französischeart	Von Löder,	Lang Röckig,	Viel Färbig,	Mit bölzen,	Weiber...
Untugent.	Hoffärtig,	Betrügerisch,	Geilsichtig,	Verschwenderisch,	Unruhig,	Aber Glaubisch,	Praller,	Veräther,	Gar Veräsherisch,	Noch...
Lieben,	Ehrlob und Rum	Den Krieg,	Das Gold,	Den Trunck,	Die Wohllust,	Köstliche Speisen	Den Adl,	Die Aufruhe,	Den Brügl,	Selbsten...
Kranckheiten,	An Verstopfung	An Ligner,	An bösser seüch	An bodogrä,	Der schwindsucht	Der Wassersucht	Den Durchbruch	In der freis,	An Reichen,	An Schr...
Ihr Land,	Ist fruchtbaar,	Wohlgearbeith	Und Wohllüstig,	Gut,	Fruchtbaar,	Bergig,	Waldich,	Und gott Reich	Voller Eis,	Ein Lieb...
Kriegs Tugente.	Groß Müthig,	Arglistig,	Fürsichtig,	Uniberwindlich	Ein See Held,	Unverzackt,	An Gestimt,	Aufriererisch	Miesamb,	Gar fa...
Gottesdienst.	Der aller beste	Gut	Etwas besser,	Noch Andächtiger	Wie der Mond	Eifrig in Glauben	Ysaubt Üllerley	Unmüeßig,	Ein Abtrüniger,	Even ein...
für Ihren Herren (Erkennen)	Einen Monarchen	Einen König,	Einen Bälerärch	Einen Käiser,	ball den ballzene	Freüe Herrschaft	Einen Erwelden	Einen Unbeliebigen	Einen Freimiligen	Ein T...
Haben Überfluß	An Früchten,	In Waren,	An Wein,	An Geträid,	An sich Weid,	An Ürtz Gruben	An Völtzwerch	In Allen,	An Immen,	Und weich...
Vertreiben (Die Zeit)	Mit Spillen,	Mit betrügen	Mit schwätzen	Mit Trincken,	Mit Arbeiten,	Mit Essen,	Mit zancken,	Mit Miessigehen	Mit schlaffen,	Mit Kr...
Mit denen Thieren (Vergleichung)	Ein Elofanthen	Ein Fuchsen,	Einen Luchsen,	Einen Löben,	Einen Pford,	Einen Ochsen,	Einen Bern,	Einen Wolffen,	Einen Esel,	Einer...
Ihr Leben Ende.	In Böth.	In Krieg,	In Kloster,	In Wein,	In Wasser.	Auf der Erd,	Im Stall,	beym Säwel,	In Schnee,	In bet...

B Business communication (see Chapter 3)

1 managing people
2 negotiating
3 socializing
4 giving presentations
5 advertising
6 applying for a job

Many people find that living or working abroad helps them to understand their own cultural background more clearly. At times we need to step back from our particular culture in order to see it to see it more impartially

As T. S. Eliot wrote in the 'Four Quartets' (1942):

We shall not cease from exploration,
And the end of all our exploring
Will be to arrive where we started
And know the place for the first time.

Exercise 36

What characteristics do you think people from other countries associate with your national culture?

Table 4.1 shows the results of a survey of 6,000 people in six different countries.

Images of people from different countries*

	Ger	Jap	USA	UK	Neth	Fra	Ita	Spa
Successful	**199**	**199**	**179**	49	45	65	49	16
Ambitious	**201**	**192**	**152**	63	40	76	49	27
Aggressive	**191**	60	**149**	131	36	66	101	66
Clever	**124**	**209**	102	80	62	93	64	44
Hard-working	**227**	**248**	72	59	67	46	42	38
Modern	118	**135**	**176**	57	57	**136**	90	33
Arrogant	**188**	33	**132**	171	39	127	66	44
Boring	124	110	69	**228**	117	69	34	48
Humorous	63	24	96	**183**	48	116	**164**	108
Helpful	99	85	99	99	90	84	**135**	99
Stylish	60	40	46	104	30	**278**	**194**	50
Lazy	21	7	35	85	35	108	**241**	**269**
Untrustworthy	71	63	94	94	47	94	**198**	**141**

*That's what the rest of us think

Table 4.1: Images of people from different countries (The European, 12–15 November 1992)

Find out what foreign business guides say about your national culture.

Interfaces

This section contains exercises ('critical incidents') based on a variety of cultural interfaces. It can't provide extensive coverage of every culture in the world, but aims to take some examples which could help to sensitize you to some of the cultural factors which you might experience, including cultures not covered here. Where possible, the situations are related to the cultural dimensions examined in Chapter 2.

When trying to understand intercultural encounters, it is important to remember that national culture is just one of the range of factors that influence what happens. Some of the key factors are illustrated in the intercultural cocktail.

Individual

Situation   Culture

Context

Critical incident 24

What do you think is happening here?

Two men meet on a plane from Tokyo to Hong Kong. Chu Hon-fai is a Hong Kong exporter who is returning from a business trip to Japan. Andrew Richardson is an American buyer on his first business trip to Hong Kong. It is a convenient meeting for them, because Mr Chu's company sells some of the same products that Mr Richardson has come to Hong Kong to buy. After a short conversation, they introduce themselves to each other.

Mr Richardson	By the way, I'm Andrew Richardson. My friends call me Andy. This is my business card.
Mr Chu	I'm David Chu. Pleased to meet you, Mr Richardson. This is my card.
Mr Richardson	No, no. Call me Andy. I think we'll be doing a lot of business together.
Mr Chu	Yes, I hope so.
Mr Richardson	(reading Mr Chu's card) Chu, Hon-fai. Hon-fai, I'll give you a call tomorrow, as soon as I get settled at my hotel.
Mr Chu	(smiling) Yes, I'll expect your call.

Comments

When these men separate, they leave each other with very different impressions of the situation. Mr Richardson is very pleased to have made the acquaintance of Mr Chu, and feels that they have got off to a very good start. They have established their relationship on a first name basis, and Mr Chu's smile seemed to indicate that he will be friendly, and easy to do business with. Mr Richardson is particularly pleased that to have treated Mr Chu in a way that shows respect for his Chinese background, by calling him Hon-fai, rather than using the Western name, David, which seemed to him to be an unnecessary imposition of Western culture.

In contrast, Mr Chu feels quite uncomfortable with Mr Richardson. He feels it will be difficult to work with him, and that Mr Richardson might be rather insensitive to cultural differences. He is particularly annoyed that Mr Richardson used his given name, Hon-fai, instead of calling him David, or Mr Chu. It was this embarrassment that caused him to smile.

(Scollon and Wong Scollon 1995: 122–3)

Critical incident 25

What do you think is happening here?

A European organization is planning a major international congress in Italy. As communication with the local organizers is almost non-existent, the group go to visit the site. They are impressed by the hospitality of the local hotel owners' association, but are worried that although the lengthy meals were most enjoyable, they are not getting very far with their business proposals. The budget is not available, and the cost of the conference venue is unclear. When one of the European group asks the Italian organizer how much the venue will cost, she replies by saying 'I'm having lunch with the head of the Chamber of Commerce tomorrow to discuss costs.' Although the committee members go home feeling frustrated, they are pleasantly surprised when the conference is a complete success, and they make a substantial profit.

Comments

For Italians, building up and looking after relationships is of utmost importance. They consider that having a meal with someone is a vital part of getting to know each other, and leads to the mutual knowledge and trust that is necessary for business to be done. In many instances, business success also depends on knowing the right people—which is why it is important for the Italian organizer to have lunch with the representative of the Chamber of Commerce. In this way the Chamber may be persuaded to become a sponsor for the event, and thus help the organizer to secure a good financial result. It is unlikely that the delegation's rather impatient approach would have produced such positive results.

As a high-context culture, in Italy oral communication is preferred to written communication, and the plans and agreements are not written down in as much detail as in lower-context cultures.

Critical incident 26

What do you think is happening here?

Senior British bankers whose businesses were taken over by German banks were interviewed about how they felt. One said: 'There is actually nothing wrong with any of my new German colleagues. They are perfectly pleasant, they work hard, they take you out for enormous meals in restaurants . . .

it's just that they are incredibly rigid. You can't deviate in any way from the corporate rules, or cut corners, even when it makes sense to do so.'

Another banker said: 'They clearly want their acquisition to be a success—you can tell that they are trying to make their British colleagues feel part of the greater company. It's just that they consistently get it wrong. We receive corporate e-mails which begin *Liebe Mitarbeiter* ('Greetings, fellow workers'), which cause a lot of amusement on the desk. And they have a different attitude to information, too. Where the British are accustomed to sharing information openly within a business, the Germans seem to believe that knowledge is power, so they can't share the knowledge, because that implies sharing power. As a result, those of us working in London are often wrong-footed by decisions taken in Germany that they haven't bothered to tell us about.

Another thing is that you can never tell them anything. German business culture doesn't allow them to say 'I didn't know that, how interesting'. So when any development happens—something unexpected—they always say '*Ja*, I knew that thing already.' It becomes highly irritating.

There are other national characteristics which exasperate British executives, and which they talk about all the time, such as '. . . the Germans' preoccupation with 10- and 20-year business plans, which they constantly update on their laptops.'

(Coleridge, Nicholas, 'We have ways of making you work',
The Sunday Telegraph, 30.8.98)

Comments

Sometimes the British staff want to 'cut corners', or ignore the rules, whereas the German managers put more emphasis on implementing company policy. The Germans rather assume that they should know the answers to every question. They also show a longer-term orientation. The communication style of the two nationalities is different, with the British requiring to be informed about everything that is happening, and not just what is strictly relevant for them. Another source of friction to the British, who are used to more informal exchanges, is the German way of greeting fellow workers, which can be seen as unnecessarily formal, and even condescending.

Critical incident 27

What do you think is happening here?

The US computer specialist Bob Moore is being taken around the Shanghai machine tool factory, which has been running for several months. He is impressed to see that the latest CAD equipment is available, but surprised that it still hasn't been installed, as it would make the whole process quicker and more efficient. On his return a month later he sees that the computers have still not been installed. As the group look around the plant again, Bob asks Mr Wang, his Chinese partner, what the problem is. Wang explains that there are frequent power cuts. Bob knows that this can't be true, since if that were the case, the rest of the plant wouldn't be working. As a result, he is annoyed to have been given such an obviously untrue answer to his perfectly reasonable question.

Comments

This incident illustrates several differences between US and Chinese ways of approaching problems. Bob concentrates on the task at hand (the technical functioning of the plant) rather than on his relationships with the staff. For them, admitting that they don't know how to install the equipment would be a loss of 'face'. In China it is very important to avoid embarrassing people, especially if their lack of skill is likely to be exposed in front of the group and a foreign visitor. It is also likely that Bob Moore's communication style is too direct for the high-context Chinese.

Table 4.2 summarizes some differences in these approaches.

Task focus (tendency in Germany)	Person focus (tendency in China)
Concentration on technical aspects of work.	Concentration on relationships with people at work.
Little small talk, distance from personal questions.	A lot of small talk, interest in personal questions.
Interest created by information, logic, technical data.	Interest created by relationships, trust, prestige.
Customers stay with the product even if the sales representative changes.	Customers stay with the sales representative even if he or she changes firm.
Results have priority over harmony and 'face'.	Results come from harmony and 'face'.
People with expert knowledge are valued. Distance from people who are not useful.	People with many relationships are valued. Distance from people who are not loyal.
Conflicts resolved by logical use of arguments, contracts, laws and compromise.	Conflicts resolved by evidence of loyalty, prestige, mediators, authority figures and new formulations.
People concentrate on the task. Friends and colleagues are kept separate.	People mix work and private life. Colleagues are also friends.

Table 4.2: Task focus and person focus   (Reisach *et al.* 1997)

Critical incident 28

What do you think is happening here?

> There seem to be problems in the German-US team. Petra Fischer feels that many problems arise from the failure of American colleagues to define clearly what everyone is supposed to do. She feels that their whole approach is very superficial, since they never seem to go into any depth when they present their new ideas. They speak positively all the time, but in the end it turns out that they really disagree. For their part, the American team members find the Germans cold, unappreciative of the work they are doing, and often very unwilling to share information.

Comments

According to Robinson and Wuebbeler (2000), who train German-US teams, there are important cultural differences in four areas. These relate to the understanding of what a team is, the approaches taken in order to motivate people, communication styles, and ways of solving problems. Their ideas can help us to understand what is happening in the critical incident.

Team

The Germans see the team as a group of individuals, each with special knowledge or skills, who are led by a competent leader. The team is clearly built into the organizational structures of the company. Once the aims have been made clear, tasks are given to the members, who generally then work on their own. The American concept is rather different. There is more frequent contact between the team members, for instance, and there are short but frequent brainstorming sessions to generate ideas. The teams form and reform as the situation demands.

Motivation

US employees expect and get more praise than their German counterparts. This can be verbal, or can take the form of special prizes, awards, or pay increases.

Communication style

According to Robinson and Wuebbeler (2000), Germans tend to communicate at work to demonstrate their knowledge and to gain respect, while the American tendency is to communicate to be liked. In presentations, the Americans concentrate on the main points, and don't go into as much analysis and detail as their German colleagues might be used to. The Americans also use the 'sandwich technique' to express criticism (i.e. the negative part is sandwiched between two positive statements). However, there is a risk that the Germans might interpret this approach as either ambiguous or dishonest.

Problem-solving

The German tendency to analyse the situation in depth before taking any action is seen negatively by the Americans, who feel that it prevents things getting done ('analysis paralysis'). The US approach is one of trying things out and seeing if they work ('trial and error').

Critical incident 29

What do you think is happening here?

> The American delegation is getting more and more frustrated with the be-haviour of the Japanese team in the negotiations about a joint venture project. The Japanese seem to spend a lot of the meetings discussing things with each other in their own language, and then keep asking the same questions over and over again. For the rest of the time they don't seem to want to talk at all, so the Americans step in to keep the discussion going. They also seem to be trying to sabotage the deal by asking for very detailed documents.

Comments

The Japanese have numerous discussions with each other. These talks are important for them, since they always aim to create a group consensus (re-flecting the high level of collectivism in their culture). This approach is not intended to be rude—indeed, the fact that they are asking questions is a sign that they are taking the negotiations seriously. The habit of repeating ques-tions comes from the fact that in Japan people often don't give a full answer the first time a question is asked. The resultant periods of silence, which tend to disturb the Americans, are a normal part of discourse in Japan, and reflect the fact that it is a high-context culture. Any attempt by the American group to keep the discussion going by joining in will be counterproductive. Nor should requests for detailed information be taken as a negative approach, but as a sign that the negotiations are going well—it suggests that key people in the company will want to see this documentation.

Critical incident 30

What do you think is happening here?

> A German manager in a Franco-German aerospace project has to deal with complaints made by the German staff about their French bosses. The French managers tell them 'If your boss takes a decision, you will simply have to accept it', or 'I will not discuss this matter with you; I will just tell you how it is.' French team workers, on the other hand, cannot under-stand how their German colleagues dare to contradict their superiors at a meeting.

Comments

This passage reflects different approaches to team decision-making in France and Germany. In France, power distance is greater than in Germany, as illustrated in Figure 3.2, p. 58. This means that whereas in Germany decision-making tends to be based on a consensus within the team, in France it may involve a boss making decisions on his or her own. The concept of 'co-determination' does not exist in France.

Research into how German and French managers see each other produced the results shown in Table 4.3.

Germans on French	French on Germans
Use too much authority.	Use too much participation.
Cannot concentrate on one problem.	Not flexible enough.
Attach too much importance to synthesis.	Too much concern for details.
Have no well-developed ideas.	No innovative ideas.
Set too much store by economic efficiency.	Set too much store by technological renown.

(Fischer 2000: 15–16)

Table 4.3: How French and German managers see each other

Critical incident 31

What do you think is happening here?

J = Japanese   F = Foreigner

F Therefore, our products meet your requirements 100%. How soon do you think you can place an order?

J Did you see the sumo wrestling last night?

F Well . . . Yes, I did. But back to our discussion, when would it be convenient . . .?

J What do you think of Jessie Takamiyama (a Hawaiian sumo wrestler)? Wasn't he terrific?

(Imai 1981: 8)

Comments

This passage reflects the indirectness of much communication in high-context Japan. Changing the subject is one way of telling the foreign businessman or woman that he doesn't want to place an order. For the Japanese partner, a direct statement would not be acceptable, since it would lead to loss of face. Other ways of saying 'no' include:

- giving a vague 'yes' or 'no'
- asking a question
- delaying answering the question
- stating regret

- using silence
- refusing to answer the question
- saying 'yes'
- apologizing.

(Gudykunst and Nishida 1994: 42–3)

Critical incident 32

What do you think is happening here?

Ms Warner is from the US, and Mr Ranjit is Indian.

Ms Warner   I thought that today we would look at the feasibility of the Ministry's proposed agribusiness project. There are several elements that need to be studied more closely before we can decide to commit any funds.

Mr Ranjit   I agree. Perhaps we could begin by discussing who the director of the project will be.

Ms Warner   That will have to be decided, of course, but first we have to see if the project will fly.

Mr Ranjit   Yes, that's my point.

Comments

Ms Warner wants to examine the substance of the Ministry's new project, to see if it is in fact a viable proposition. Mr Ranjit is also very interested in determining the project's viability, but not by examining its substance; he will decide according to who is put in charge of the project. That is, if someone with the right sort of influence and authority is put in charge, it will be a sign that the Ministry takes the project seriously (regardless of the eventual outcome). Similarly, if a minor official with no particular clout is given the programme, it's a good bet that the enterprise will never get off the ground (once again, the substance notwithstanding). The American inclination is to assume that government programmes are selected and/or created based on their inherent validity, and that they are undertaken on the assumption that they meet some pressing national or regional need. In other words, personalities should not play any part in the matter, since civil servants should be above subjective considerations. But Mr Ranjit knows his country and its customs: when a pressing national need squares off against a pressing personal agenda, there is no true contest. This doesn't have to mean that civil servants in India are only in the game to advance their selfish interests; instead, it may mean that they assume—perhaps naively—that their own interests, and those of their constituents, are one and the same.

(Storti 1994: 55, 84)

Further reading

Interfaces

There is an excellent book which looks at management in Britain and Germany in considerable depth. It is based on important research into the behaviour of middle managers, and is written by an Anglo-German team: **Stewart, R., J-L., Barsoux , H-D., Ganter,** and **P. Walgenbach.** 1994. *Managing in Britain and Germany.* Basingstoke: Macmillan.

A classic introduction to the Japanese, and to doing business in Japan, is **Hall, E. T.** and **M. Reed.** 1987. *Hidden Differences: Doing business with the Japanese.* New York: Anchor Books.

Useful sources of more critical incidents are:

Cushner, K. and **R. Brislin.** 1996. (2nd edn.). *Intercultural Interactions.* Thousand Oaks: Sage.

Storti, C. 1994. *Cross-cultural Dialogues.* Yarmouth: Intercultural Press.

5 GOING FURTHER

Intercultural training

Training methods

Briefings
Briefings concentrate on the transfer of information about cultures—people from the target culture, or who have experience of it, are often invited to give a lecture or workshop. Training remains on the cognitive level.

Using culture models
Culture models like those developed by Hofstede and Trompenaars can be used as a basis for training. Participants are encouraged to use the models as tools in order to help them understand intercultural encounters.

Culture assimilator training
Sets of critical incidents are used to encourage participants to interpret situations from the perspective of the target culture.

Interaction training
Case studies and role plays are used to simulate interaction with people from the target culture. This training is often carried out by teams of trainers, with the help of a facilitator who is from, or is familiar with the culture of the participants, and a country specialist who knows or is from the target culture.

Designing training programmes
The following factors should be considered when planning intercultural training:

What are the parameters?

- What resources are available?
- Can staff be given time off work for training?
- Who is going to be responsible for checking quality?
- Are there alternatives to training (for example, the employment of foreign employees, requiring relevant experience from new staff)?

What are the needs of the company?

- Which cultures are they concerned with? Is training culture-general, or culture-specific?
- In what situations will staff be involved in intercultural interactions (e.g. in negotiating)?

Who should take part in the training programme?

- Are the participants motivated?
- Is training for the partner and children to be included?
- Are the participants multipliers who will pass on their knowledge to other members of the company?

Why do the participants need intercultural training?

- Are they going to work abroad?
- Are they going to work in international teams in their own country?
- Will they need intercultural skills now, or at a later stage?

What previous knowledge do participants have?

- Have they taken part in other training programmes?
- Have they lived or worked abroad before?

What methods are suitable?

- Briefings.
- Culture models (for example, Hofstede's dimensions).
- Culture assimilator training.
- Interaction training.

Are there clear and realistic aims to the training?

- Have the needs and previous experience of the participants been taken into account?
- Can the aims be realized in the time available?

Are the trainers properly qualified?

- Do the trainers have a knowledge of the target culture?
- Do the trainers have a knowledge of the target business sector?
- Have the trainers been trained to train?

Is there adequate follow-up to the training?

- Is there assessment of the results of the training programme?
- Is there support for trainees after the programme?

(Adapted from Gibson 1997: 311–18)

Sources of further information

SIETAR

The Society for Intercultural Education, Training and Research, with groups throughout the world, is the largest interdisciplinary organization in the field. Activities include building networks of interculturalists, organizing seminars, conferences, and workshops, and producing publications.

www.sietarusa.org

www.sietar-europa.org

DELTA Intercultural Academy

The DELTA Academy is an intercultural forum on the internet. Members have access to a range of services connected with intercultural issues. Forums and chat rooms make it possible for participants to exchange experience and expertise. Resources on intercultural issues can be downloaded from the following site: www.dialogin.com

Further reading

Tomalin, B. and **S. Stempleski.** 1993. *Cultural Awareness.* Oxford: Oxford University Press.

Utley, D. 2000. *The Culture Pack: Intercultural communication resources for trainers.* York: York Associates.

GLOSSARY

ATTRIBUTION: attempts to explain the behaviour of others

CHANNEL: a medium for communication

COLLECTIVISM: a system in which people are integrated into strong groups

CONTEXT: the information surrounding an event

CULTURE: a shared system of attitudes, beliefs, values, and behaviour

CULTURE SHOCK: a negative reaction to living in a new culture

DIRECTNESS: the open communication of meaning

DIVERSITY: a variety of different people or things

EXPATRIATE: someone living in a foreign country

FACE: the exterior dignity of a person

FEMININITY: where the roles of women and men overlap

HIGH CONTEXT: where information is transmitted implicitly

INDIRECTNESS: the implicit communication of meaning

INDIVIDUALISM: a system in which ties between individuals are loose

INTERCULTURAL: between cultures

LONG-TERM ORIENTATION: a concern with the future, rather than with the present or short term

LOW CONTEXT: where information is transmitted explicitly

MASCULINITY: where the roles of men and women are distinct

MESSAGE: what is communicated between the sender and receiver

MONOCHRONIC: doing one thing at a time

PARTICULARISM: where behaviour is guided by specific circumstances, rather than by rules

PERCEPTION: an awareness of what is happening in our environment

PERSON-RELATED: concentrated on people rather than on things or tasks

POLYCHRONIC: doing many things at one time

POWER DISTANCE: the acceptance of an unequal distribution of power

RECEIVER: the person getting the message

SENDER/SOURCE: the person from whom the message comes

SHORT-TERM ORIENTATION: concern with the present and with the near future

STEREOTYPE: the fixed idea or image that people have of a type of person or thing, which in reality is not always true

SYNERGY: where the combined effect is more than the sum of the individual parts

TASK-RELATED: a concern for tasks and things rather than with people

UNCERTAINTY AVOIDANCE: the extent to which people feel threatened by the unknown

UNIVERSALISM: where behaviour is guided by rules rather than specific circumstances

RECOMMENDED READING

As interest in the field of intercultural communication grows, so more and more books are published on the subject. Good starting points for those interested in the subject are:

Brake, T., D. Walker, and **T. Walker.** 1995. *Doing Business Internationally: The Guide to Cross-cultural Success.* New York: Irwin.

Trompenaars, F. and **C. Hampden-Turner.** 1997 (2nd edn.). *Riding the Waves of Culture.* Hemel Hempstead: Nicholas Brealey.

Those with a more serious interest will find it essential to read:

Adler, N. 1997. *International Dimensions of Organizational Behavior.* Cincinnati: ITP.

Hofstede, G. 1991. *Cultures and Organizations.* London: McGraw Hill.

Useful readers with extracts from key sources, which make a good introduction to the field, are:

Bennett, M. (ed.). 1998. *Basic Concepts of Intercultural Communication.* Yarmouth: Intercultural Press.

Samovar, L. R. and **R. Porter.** (eds.). 1995 (7th edn.). *Intercultural Communication: A Reader.* Belmont: Wadsworth.

A publisher specializing in books on intercultural issues is:

Intercultural Press

www.interculturalpress.com

BIBLIOGRAPHY

Adler, N. 1997. *International Dimensions of Organizational Behavior.* Cincinnati: ITP.

Ansari, K. H. and **J. Jackson.** 1995. *Managing Cultural Diversity at Work.* London: Kogan Page.

Axtell, R. 1991. *Gestures.* New York: John Wiley.

Bennett, J. *et al.* 1998. *Doing Effective Presentations in an Intercultural Setting.* Vienna: Ueberreuter.

Bennett, M. (ed.). 1998. *Basic Concepts of Intercultural Communication.* Yarmouth: Intercultural Press.

Brake, T., D. Walker, and **T. Walker.** 1995. *Doing Business Internationally: the Guide to Cross-cultural Success.* New York: Irwin.

Brislin, R. 1981. *Cross-cultural Encounters: Face-to-Face Interaction.* Boston: Allyn and Bacon.

Brislin, R. 1993. *Understanding Culture's Influence on Behavior.* Orlando: Harcourt Brace.

Casse, P. and **Deol, S.** 1985. *Managing Intercultural Negotiations.* Washington: SIETAR International.

Clackworthy, D., A. Moosmüller, and **L. Beerman.** 1995. *Signposts from a Cultural Interaction Training Project.* Munich: Siemens; Fishkill: IBM; Tokyo: Toshiba.

Claes, M. 2000. *Presentation Skills in an International Setting.* Bath: LTS and SIETAR.

Collett, P. 1993. *Foreign Bodies: A Guide to European Mannerisms.* London: Simon and Schuster.

Copeland, L. and **L. Briggs.** 1985. *Going International.* New York: Random House.

Cushner, K. and **R. Brislin.** 1996. (2nd edn.). *Intercultural Interactions.* Thousand Oaks: Sage.

Dahl, Ø. 1994. 'When the future comes from behind. Malagasy and other time concepts and some consequences for communication' in D. Marsh and S. Liis. *Europe on the Move: fusion or fission?* Jyväskylä: SIETAR Europa.

Fischer, M. 2000. 'The Uneasy Road to Cross-Border Co-operation and Mergers.' *SIETAR Europa Newsletter* 1/2000: 15–16.

Francesco, A. M. and **B. A. Gold.** 1997. *International Organizational Behavior.* Upper Saddle River: Prentice Hall.

Furnham, A. and **S. Bochner.** 1986. *Culture Shock.* London: Routledge.

Garratt-Gnann, N., N. Haines, and **C. Vignal.** 1997. 'Efficient Managers— How are they perceived in a worldwide operating company?' in P. Crubézy, K. Cresson, and K. Dameron (eds.): *Images, Cultures, Communication.* Paris: SIETAR Europa.

Gibson, R. 1997. 'Zur Auswahl von Sprachen und interkulturellem Training' in A. Clemont and W. Schmeisser (eds.): *Internationales Personen-management* Munich: Vahlen.

Gibson, R. (ed.). 1998. *International Communication in Business: Theory and Practice.* Sternenfels: Verlag Wissenschaft und Praxis.

Gudykunst, W. B. and **S. Ting-Toomey.** 1988. *Culture and Interpersonal Communication.* Newbury Park: Sage.

Gudykunst, W. B. 1994. *Bridging Differences: Effective Intergroup Communication.* Thousand Oaks: Sage.

Gudykunst, W. B. and **T. Nishida.** 1994. *Bridging Japanese/North American Differences.* Thousand Oaks: Sage.

Guirdham, M. 1999. *Communicating across Cultures.* Houndmills: Macmillan.

Hall, E. 1959. *The Silent Language.* New York: Doubleday.

Hall, E. 1966. *The Hidden Dimension.* New York: Doubleday Anchor Books.

Hall, E. 1976. *Beyond Culture.* New York: Doubleday.

Hampden-Turner C. and **F. Trompenaars.** 1993. *The Seven Cultures of Capitalism.* New York: Doubleday.

Hampden-Turner, C. and **F. Trompenaars.** 2000. *Building Cross-Cultural Competence.* Chichester: John Wiley.

Handy, C. 1990. *Inside Organizations.* London: BBC.

Harris, P. R. and R. T. Moran. 1991. (3rd edn.). *Managing Cultural Differences.* Houston: Gulf.

Hickson, D. and D. Pugh. 1995. *Management Worldwide.* Harmondsworth: Penguin.

Hickson, D. (ed.) 1997. *Exploring Management across the World: Selected Readings.* Harmondsworth: Penguin.

Hoecklin, L. 1994. *Managing Cultural Differences.* Wokingham: Addison Wesley.

Hofstede, G. 1980. *Culture's Consequences: International Differences in Work-related Values.* Beverly Hills: Sage.

Hofstede, G. 1991. *Cultures and Organizations.* London: McGraw Hill.

Imai, M. 1981. *16 Ways to Avoid Saying No.* Tokyo: Nihon Keizer Shimbun.

Jandt, F. 1995. *Intercultural Communication: an Introduction.* Thousand Oaks: Sage.

Kale, S. H. 1995. 'Grouping Euroconsumers: a culture-based clustering approach.' *Journal of International Marketing* 3: 1.

Kluckhohn, F. and F. Strodtbeck. 1961. *Variations in Value Orientations.* Evanston: Row Petersen.

Landis, D. and R. Bhagat. 1996. (2nd edn.) *Handbook of Intercultural Training.* Thousand Oaks: Sage.

Laurent, A. 1993. 'The cultural diversity of Western conceptions of management.' *International Studies of Management and Organization* 13/1–2: 75–96.

Lewis, R. 1996. *When Cultures Collide.* London: Nicholas Brealey.

Marx, E. 1999. *Breaking through Culture Shock.* London: Nicholas Brealey.

Mead, R. 1998. (2nd edn.). *International Management.* Oxford: Blackwell.

Mole, J. 1990. *Mind your Manners.* London: The Industrial Society.

Moran, R., D. Braaten, and D. Walsh. 1994. *International Business Case Studies for the Multicultural Marketplace.* Houston: Gulf.

Oberg, K. 1960. 'Cultural shock: adjustment to new cultural environments'. *Practical Anthropology* 7.

O'Connor, P., A. Pilbeam, and F. Scott-Barrett. 1992. *Negotiating.* Harlow: Longman.

Pauwels, M. 2000. 'The use of imagery and symbols on the internet—intercultural aspects' in Lynch, D. and A. Pilbeam. *Heritage and Progress: from the Past to the Future in Intercultural Understanding.* Bath: LTS & SIETAR Europa.

Reisach, U., T. Tauber, and X. Yuan. 1997. *China—Wirtschaftspartner zwischen Wunsch und Wirklichkeit.* Vienna: Ueberreuter.

Robinson, H. and R. Wuebbeler. 2000. 'Teaming with trouble—Konflikt-potentiale in deutsch-amerikanischen Teams.' *SIETAR Deutschland Newsletter* 1/2000: 16–18.

Samovar, L. and R. Porter. (eds.) 1995. (7th edn.) *Intercultural Communication: a Reader.* Belmont: Wadsworth.

Schneider, S. and J-L. Barsoux. 1997. *Managing across Cultures.* London: Prentice Hall.

Scollon, R. and S. Wong Scollon. 1995. *Intercultural Communication.* Oxford: Blackwell.

Stewart, R., J-L. Barsoux, H. D. Ganter, and P. Walgenbach. 1994. *Managing in Britain and Germany.* Houndmills: Macmillan.

Storti, C. 1990. *The Art of Crossing Cultures.* Yarmouth: Intercultural Press.

Storti, C. 1994. *Cross-cultural Dialogues.* Yarmouth: Intercultural Press.

Tannen, D. 1995. *Talking from 9 to 5.* London: Virago.

Tomalin, B. and S. Stempleski. 1993. *Cultural Awareness.* Oxford: Oxford University Press.

Triandis, H. 1975. 'Culture training, cognitive complexity and interpersonal attitudes' in R. Brislin *et al.* (eds.). 1997. *Cross-cultural Perspectives on Learning.* Beverly Hills: Sage.

Trompenaars, F. and C. Hampden-Turner. 1997. (2nd edn.). *Riding the Waves of Culture.* London: Nicholas Brealey.

Usunier, J.-C. 1993. *International Marketing: a Cultural Approach.* Hemel Hempstead: Prentice Hall.

Utley, D. 2000. *The Culture Pack: Intercultural Communication Resources for Trainers.* York: York Associates.

Verluyten, P. 1999. 'Conflict avoidance in Thailand.' Paper presented at the ENCoDE conference, 1999.

Zaninelli, S. 1994. 'Vier Schritte eines integrierten Trainingsansatzes am Beispiel des interkulturellen Trainings Bundesrepublik Deutschland—Vereinigte Staaten' in *Interkulturelle Kommunikation und Interkulturelles Training.* Institut für Auslandsbeziehungen.

INDEX OF EXERCISES
AND CRITICAL INCIDENTS

This index helps you to find out more about particular dimensions or specific cultures. The numbers refer to the exercise and/or critical incident in which the dimension or culture is dealt with.

INDEX

All countries mentioned in the text can be found in the index of exercises and critical incidents on pp. 107–8. Page references to the Glossary (page 99) are indicated by g.